Henry Parker Fellows

Boating Trips on New England Rivers

Henry Parker Fellows

Boating Trips on New England Rivers

ISBN/EAN: 9783744791519

Printed in Europe, USA, Canada, Australia, Japan

Cover: Foto ©Andreas Hilbeck / pixelio.de

More available books at **www.hansebooks.com**

BOATING TRIPS

ON

NEW ENGLAND RIVERS

BY
HENRY PARKER FELLOWS

ILLUSTRATED BY WILLIS H. BEALS

BOSTON
CUPPLES, UPHAM, AND COMPANY
Old Corner Bookstore
1884

To my friend C. C. POWERS, Esq., who will, I imagine, take more pleasure reading between the lines than any one else can possibly take in reading the narratives themselves, I inscribe our Inland Voyage and the Trip on the Nashua.

To E. T. SLOCUM, Esq., who will, I am sure, if no one else does, read with some degree of interest the lines of our experiences on the Housatonic, I dedicate our Autumn Cruise.

PREFACE.

It is the author's purpose, in the following pages, to describe trips he has taken in a skiff, from summer to summer, on one or another of our home rivers.

The initial article appeared, in part, originally in the Boston Courier, and the Cruise on the Housatonic in the Springfield Republican; while the trip on the Nashua is now published for the first time.

H. P. F.

CONTENTS.

I. AN INLAND VOYAGE ON THE SUDBURY, CONCORD, AND MERRIMAC RIVERS.

CHAPTER I.
	Page
SOUTHVILLE. — CONCORD	17

CHAPTER II.
CONCORD	33

CHAPTER III.
CONCORD. — NEWBURYPORT	41
PRACTICAL SUGGESTIONS	54

II. AN AUTUMN CRUISE ON THE HOUSATONIC.

CHAPTER I.
PITTSFIELD. — LEE	61

CHAPTER II.
LEE. — GREAT BARRINGTON	77

CHAPTER III.
GREAT BARRINGTON. — KENT	94

CHAPTER IV.
KENT. — STRATFORD	112

III. THE NASHUA RIVER.

CHAPTER I.

West Boylston. — Lancaster   Page 129

CHAPTER II.

Lancaster. — Groton   146

CHAPTER III.

Groton. — Nashua   159

LIST OF ILLUSTRATIONS.

	Page
BRIDGE AT SOUTHVILLE	18
STONE'S BRIDGE	27
SHERMAN'S BRIDGE	31
ON THE SUDBURY	32
SOUTH BRIDGE AT CONCORD	33
THE OLD MANSE	37
THE WAYSIDE	39
THE OLD NORTH BRIDGE	42
BRIDGE AT NORTH BILLERICA	46
HAWTHORNE'S WRITING DESK	64
POMEROY'S LOWER MILL. PITTSFIELD	66
LENOX FURNACE	74
THE HOUSATONIC FROM FERN CLIFF	78
TANGLEWOOD	80
SOUTH GLENDALE	86
OLD HOUSE AT GREAT BARRINGTON	90
GREAT BARRINGTON	94
A CRAZY BRIDGE	95
AT FALLS VILLAGE	103
WEST CORNWALL BRIDGE	108
LOVER'S LEAP	117
WEST BOYLSTON	131
HOLBROOK'S MILL	133
CANAL AT WEST BOYLSTON	135
OLD BRIDGE AT BOYLSTON	137
MILL AT SOUTH LANCASTER	141

	Page
GROTON	164
BRIDGE AT PEPPERELL	168
MAIN STREET BRIDGE, NASHUA	173
JUNCTION OF NASHUA AND MERRIMAC	175

MAPS.

	Page
THE SUDBURY, CONCORD, AND NASHUA RIVERS. (Frontispiece).	
THE MERRIMAC FROM LOWELL TO NEWBURYPORT	51
THE HOUSATONIC RIVER	63
THE HOUSATONIC FROM MONUMENT MOUNTAIN TO KONKAPOT RIVER	99
THE NASHUA FROM WEST BOYLSTON TO STILL RIVER VILLAGE	153

AN INLAND VOYAGE

ON THE

SUDBURY, CONCORD, AND MERRIMAC

RIVERS.

CHAPTER I.

SOUTHVILLE. — CONCORD.

THE source of the Sudbury River is, I was about to say, among the clouds. It appears upon earth, however, in the form of two rivulets, one of which flows from Whitehall Pond, a beautiful sheet of water in Hopkinton, and the other, beginning from indeterminate places in Westborough, joins the Hopkinton branch just above Southville. Which is the Sudbury River we leave Hopkinton and Westborough to settle between them, although perhaps ere this, for aught we know, they may, in order to avoid controversy, have divided the honor. After the junction the river flows in an easterly direction to Ashland, and thence pursues a generally northeasterly course, until with the Assabet, in Concord, it forms the Concord River.

It was the desire of the writer and a friend in taking a boating trip down the river to obtain a rowboat at the pond at Hopkinton; but it appeared to be difficult to procure a suitable craft, and it seemed very doubtful whether the branch from the lake, in its several miles of flow to the other branch, was navigable; so we concluded to take a skiff to Southville and start from there.

By virtue of an order of Mr. Hobart, station-master of the Boston and Albany Railroad, we had our skiff put on board the baggage car of the seven A.M. train from Boston, upon the payment of one extra fare, seventy cents. We arrived at Southville soon after eight o'clock, and were obliged to wait in the station a couple of hours on

Bridge at Southville

account of a severe thunder shower. As the clouds were breaking away, we carried our boat on a wheelbarrow to a stone bridge, with a single small arch, about two hundred feet from the station, and launched her on the right-hand side, and, having embarked with the baggage, pulled down stream. The river was barely wide enough to allow free play to the oars. The water was sufficiently deep, however, though the river most of the way was filled with beds of long, limp, gently winding blades of grass. Halting at a leaf-embowered bend midway between Southville and Cordaville, we partook of lunch in a beautiful stretch of sloping woods amid moss-gray bowlders, and at high noon were again on our way.

We soon pulled over a pond and came to the mill-dam at Cordaville. The bed of the river below the dam was dry, so, disembarking, we carried our boat around the mill on the left-hand side (left, facing down stream), and deposited her at the bottom of a deep tail-race, and patiently waited for the mill to begin work so that we might float away on the waste water. Soon we heard the machinery in motion and quickly the water rose in the canal and soon carried us forward under an arched stone bridge into the river. We then had rather difficult work in pushing and poling for about a mile until we came to the dam at Chattanooga, having unwisely hurried on in the shallow channel instead of waiting for the waste water from the mill to raise the stream. We were compelled to pull the boat over several rocky places, however, which are impassable in a boat at all times, except, perhaps, when the water is high, as in the spring. As we were pushing through one place where the stream was completely blockaded with overhanging bushes, Bow found just beneath his hand a bird's nest in which were three light blue eggs.

We hauled up near the sluice-way in front of the mill

and carried our boat on a wheelbarrow about three hundred feet over a road past the right of the mill, where the proprietor, Mr. Aldrich, who had kindly loaned us the barrow, came out with his boys and wished us good luck on our voyage. We pulled under a bridge of the Boston and Albany Railroad, which crosses the river just below the mill, and had a delightful row in a narrow, deep channel with a fine current, until we came to a deserted dam. We pulled to shore on the left-hand side and hauled the boat over the framework of the sluice-way to the embankment, and thence into the canal below, where, in still water under arching trees which cast deep shadows, we poled the boat for about a hundred yards until we emerged into a pond. Crossing this pond we came to a low dam. We pulled the boat over the middle of the dam in a few minutes, but then were obliged to get out and drag her through several gravelly shallows two or three hundred feet to a bridge, and thence had difficult navigation a short distance further, until we entered the pond at Ashland.

About six o'clock we came to the dam and stopped on the right-hand side thereof, at the head of the sluice-way. Below the dam is a series of extensive buildings which were intended to be used as print-works, an industry that, on account of the injurious effect of the dyes upon the stream, unfortunately had to be abandoned, when Boston took the Sudbury River as a source of its water supply.

Only a portion of the premises is now occupied as a thread-mill. Below the dam, for nearly a third of a mile, the bed of the river was so shallow that it was impossible to float the boat, so we endeavored to procure a conveyance to carry the boat around by the road.

While waiting on the bank a number of Ashland gamins crowded around and were altogether a saucy lot. We could obtain no conveyance of any kind, so, as it was growing dark, and we wished to get further down stream away from the Ashland gamins, to pitch our tent, we carried the boat through the mill-yard, and with friendly assistance after a while put her into the water below the first road bridge. The stream was still very shallow, however, so we alternately carried along the bank or dragged the boat through shallows to a place about half a mile below the dam. When embarked and once more able to row, it was quite dark. Pulling on, we several times got into wrong channels, and soon found that we were in a labyrinth, in which it was as difficult to find an outlet as it is to trace one's way through the puzzling mazes of Rosamond's Bower. In the course of a half-hour, however, after meeting many obstructions, we passed under a bridge and continued on along past several houses, which we afterward discovered were in the lower part of Ashland. As we rowed by the last house a little girl cried out in the darkness, " Halloo! who are you?" We said. " Boating on the river," and bade her good-night.

She responded, " Good-night," and added, in tender treble, the kindly invocation, —

>"May you sleep tight,
> Where the bugs don't bite!"

Immediately below, we pulled under a bridge, but after rowing on about half a mile we found that we were entangled in a multitude of winding and shallowing bayous, with long marshy grass on every side and a causeway in front, and merely a glimmering landscape around. We were indeed completely baffled, and as it was eleven o'clock we put back to the bridge, and after vainly trying to get directions for our course we concluded to stop at one of the houses. The young man who acted as our cicerone talked the true middle-of-England dialect, as it appears in Griffith Gaunt and Nicholas Nickleby. His peculiar pronunciation of " meestur " was very pleasing, and especially pleasant the tones of his voice as he rapped up Mr. Pratt, who, in most hospitable fashion, as we had been assured would be the case, took us in and rid us of the chief difficulty of our situation until the morrow.

Upon crossing the bridge early in the morning to embark again, we readily discovered the cause of our erroneous wandering the night before. The course of the river was very similar to the shape of the letter V. As we proceeded along we had come to the bridge at the apex of the V, as it were, and of course, naturally enough, in the darkness, immediately rowed under it. The river, however, instead of flowing under the bridge, turns sharply to the northeast, and we should have rowed up the other side of the V, as it were.

In a few minutes we were rowing in front of the bridge, and soon left it in the rear. In about a third of a mile a low dam compelled us to make a very short carry on the left side, and we then entered the first of the city reservoirs. We hauled over a low dam at the end of the first pond on the left, a very easy obstacle to pass, and after a pull over another pond with the Boston and Albany Railroad on our right, we came to a low causeway, over which we hauled the boat, and then pulled through a long stretch of water to a very high dam, guarded on the right by a small but very artistic gate-house, wherein are the gates for regulating the supply of water, and several hydrometers. The row in the deep water basin under the hot sun had been pretty warm, so we lingered in the shade of the gate-house on the dam before undertaking the fresh task of getting the boat over. It was hard work to pull the boat to the top of the embankment on the right of the dam (which is about twenty-five feet high), over the heavy masonry, at an angle of about forty-five degrees. The descent, however, on the lower side, was comparatively easy, and we were soon pulling across the last reservoir to dam number one.

Bow was quite surprised to ascertain that number one was the last dam, there having been much talk about dam number one, dam number two, and dam number three; he naturally supposing that number one was the first, instead of the last, of the series. We found the water of the last pond filled with innumerable fine particles of the vegetable matter which has been the occasion of so much disturbance to the citizens of Boston and their water-board, from time to time, for the past several years. The phenomenon appearing in only one pond, and there developed to such an extent, is certainly very remarkable. Experts have declared, however, that the matter does not impair the purity of the water, though we did not care to drink it.

Dam number one we found almost as difficult to get by as dam number two. We carried over on the right and lowered the boat over quite a high stone wall below the gate-house into the river. Only one hundred and forty thousand gallons of water are let through the dam each day to supply the mill at Saxonville, and consequently the river-bed was quite shallow. Stroke kept in the boat, and after poling by a number of rocks in a few minutes reached comparatively clear water. The going continued to improve, and ere long we came to the camp-meeting ground at South Framingham. Rowing on through a long, narrow pond we came to a short, low dam. We let the boat float over with the fall of water under a house at the middle of the dam, and below had to get out at brief intervals and pull over several gravelly shallows. The going soon became good, except at rare intervals where a shallow compelled us to push along or get out of the boat and haul through. The water was clear, however, and the banks lined with trees, and, except when we came to an arched stone bridge and saw some men mowing, our course for about two miles was along a narrow, winding stream, exceedingly pleasant. We passed a number of piles of stones heaped up in the form of round bee-hives; and on one a water-snake (I think he must have been asleep), threatened with an oar, maintained his position until thrust off. After a while the river wound in more open country and then again amid a hilly country with thick woods on every side. It was noon and the sun was shining hot. Not a breath of air was stirring, but we kept on, wishing to get below Saxonville at as early an hour as we could and go into camp.

Emerging from the woody banks, we crossed a pond and came to a deserted dam, which is about two miles above Saxonville. The dam is broken on the right side with the water at the same level below as above, and we found that we had just room enough to pass between two iron axles, each surmounted by a huge iron cog-wheel, high in air, that formerly composed part of the machinery of a grist and lumber mill. We pulled over the buoyed race-course on the upper part of the Saxonville pond, and at the ice-house a huge cake of ice was thrown into the pond for our benefit, where it looked very odd floating about in midsummer. We soon came in sight of the mill and houses at Saxonville, and about two o'clock hauled ashore on the left-hand side of the dam and had our boat transported through the town by the Adams Express, and put into the water near a livery-stable by the railroad-station.

Saxonville is a very fine specimen of the New-England manufacturing village. It is grouped in very picturesque fashion around the end of the pond, and looks extremely neat and thrifty. There is a boat-house on the pond and many boats. A road has been cut through the woods on the north side of the pond. This improvement, as well as many others, is due to the public spirit of Mr. Simpson, who, from the constant rumor of his name, is evidently the presiding genius of the town.

We found the stream below Saxonville shallow and filled with many rocks. The water was clogged with all sorts of impurities from the woolen-mill, and so muddy that we could only guess at obstructions. A violent gust of wind, preceding an impending shower, which luckily for us, however, did not fall, drove us down stream at first at a rapid rate. For about a mile we were seldom able to row, and although compelled most of the time to push along with the oars, and often meeting apparently impassable obstructions, very fortunately were not once obliged, as we often feared we should be, to get out of the boat. The stream itself was disgusting, though lined much of the way on the right by a very pretty, wooded bank. The oars in poling sank through thick, yellow water deep into oozy beds of yielding, slippery slime, and the odor stirred up by the action was foul and miasmatic. Indeed, neither Styx nor Phlegethon, I suspect, is half so bad.

After an hour or more of progress in this wretched fashion the water grew deeper, while the banks were often

Stones Bridge

quite abrupt and well wooded. A prostrate tree now and then threatened to entangle us in its branches. We wondered how we should be able to get by one, until we found a natural arch in a huge branch that lay upon the water, through which, when the way seemed most beset with perplexities, we passed in triumph. The river ran into many curving recesses where the water looked heavy and somnolent, and we were glad indeed, after a while, upon passing through an open meadow, to arrive at Stone's

Bridge. The bridge is only a mile from the village, but the river in its tortuous course makes a circuit of more than three miles thither. At one place the neck between the banks is only a few rods across, and if one could only discover the spot from the river a short carry would save a row of nearly a mile.

A low hill to the right of Stone's Bridge commands a fine prospect. The view of the river winding along to the north through the broad, level Wayland meadows is especially beautiful.

The river below the bridge is comparatively free from impurity. A cluster of thick grass occasionally blocked up the river from bank to bank, and hindered the free motion of the boat, without, however, materially delaying our progress. On the left are several hillsides, covered with trees, with curving meadows between. We spread our tent on an old road which ran along the side of one of the hills, under the trees, and stretching ourselves out upon the ground, we watched the moving leaves shadowed in silhouette by the glow of the dying fire against the canvas, and amid the mournful croaking of an army of frogs in the river below, and the strange, unearthly sounds of the woods around, we fell into slumber deep and unbroken until nine o'clock on the morrow.

Soon after starting Monday morning, we came to a place where the river was completely blockaded by dense masses of grass and rushes and lily-pads. Rowing was very slow and tedious for about a quarter of a mile. By and by, however, the channel grew clearer, and then the river, entirely free from impurity, began to wind in serpentine mazes through level meadows. The shores were lined with grass sedges and bordered with lilies, white and fragrant, while on every broad, leafy pad sat a frog. Here was, I think, the paradise of Batrachians. They sat in silence and stared at us with solemn gaze as we floated by. Even a thrust of the oar did not suffice to disturb the judicial serenity of some old croaker, who merely winked as the oar approached, or reluctantly abandoned his position as he was swept off at the end of a stroke. But the pond-lilies were indeed most wondrous, especially as we came to the head of Long Pond, just above Wayland. Upon either shore the spotless white array, immaculate in purity, stretched along as far as one could see, and the air was filled with their delicious fragrance. As we neared the end of the pond, the view of the hills encircling the valley at a distance was very fine. Beyond the broad meadows the slopes looked extremely rich and luxuriant.

We halted at the Wayland bridge for a short time, and then rowed past a bank lined with enormous cat-o'-nine-tails that would have delighted lovers of modern art in nature, and then under the bridge of the Massachusetts Central Railroad to the Sudbury-Wayland bridge. Below this bridge the river wound in continuous crooked folds through a wide expanse of marshes. The channel was marked on either side by lines of grass, and below was often filled with waving weeds. Occasionally the stream was completely clogged with grass, so that it was hard work to pull through, and at intervals the stream flowed through a small pond-like stretch of water. Altogether the scene was quite tropical, the luxuriant vegetation of the wide marsh contrasting strangely in the quiet noonday with the varied upland scenery on every side.

As we drew near the end of the meadows, Bow espied at the beginning of a little pond into which the river opened a huge black object, which we almost immediately discovered to be the head of a monstrous water-snake. He quickly saw us too, and as we ceased rowing he began to move. We were for a moment in grave apprehension as to his intentions, and were greatly relieved to see him direct his course toward the reeds at the margin of the water. He turned around and looked at us during his slow retreat, renewing our apprehension each time, but continued on, one immense fold following another, until he disappeared in the marsh. He must have been seven or eight feet long, and tapered sharply at the tail. We heard him for several minutes, splashing through the reeds, and saw the reeds, disturbed by his sinuous winding, moving some distance away from the channel before we ventured to proceed.

We soon came to another bridge, and about half a mile

below drew to shore and passed the afternoon beneath the refreshing shade of some trees. Then late in the day we rowed on by some very pretty wooded hillsides, and in the course of an hour came to Sherman's Bridge, at North Sudbury. Upon the left of the river the country slopes

up to the town in broad and fertile tracts, and to the left of the bridge and just beyond rises a hill gracefully picturesque. On the right, the sloping banks were ornamented with clumps of trees, while the bridge itself accented a river scene rich in beauty.

About half a mile below the bridge we put ashore at a point which juts into the river on the right, and found admirable camping ground in an open forest alongside a grassy road that led up from the river. While eating supper in dusky shadows by the waning fire, drops of rain began to rattle on the dry leaves around. Retiring to the tent we soon heard the roar of the storm above. At frequent intervals the tree-tops, shaken by the wind, sent down a shower of large drops that battered musically upon the canvas. The rain poured in torrents all night and the greater part of the following morning.

On the Sudbury.

CHAPTER II.

CONCORD.

OUR camping place was within the borders of Concord. Walden Pond was accessible, and not far distant; but we did not care to undertake a tramp there in the wet. We got under way again on the river about the middle of the afternoon. A few strokes carried us to

Fair Haven Bay, where hills rise on every side, shutting in the prospect with walls of living green. The river is here, indeed, wild and picturesque, and was a favorite resort of Thoreau. After a long, hard pull against a strong head wind, we came to the old South Bridge at Concord. The river, here and below, was sluggish, and as we continued on we caught a glimpse, in the quiet evening, of that tranquillity for which the town itself is noted, which it undoubtedly derives from the river. The water was like glass; the freighted clouds hung in solemn masses in the west, and the sunlight poured in golden floods over earth and sky. Pulling under the stone bridge, we came to the Grand Canal of Concord, and met several rowboats flying along the watery way, and among others a dark-blue yawl with a crew of two young ladies, who pulled a gentlemanly coxswain with a graceful yet effective stroke, that was, I suspect, the product of much patient coaching.

The village is situated on the east side of the river. The shore at the rear of the gardens of the houses on the bank was lined with every kind of rowing craft. The river is indeed the greatest part of Concord. Just below the bridge of the Lowell Railroad, the Assabet joins the Sudbury, the two streams forming the Concord River. At the junction is a little promontory, called Egg Rock, where we landed, as the shadows of evening began to gather. We pitched the tent near the top of the elevation, and after a hastily improvised supper stretched ourselves out upon the hard ground for slumber. A multitude of frogs in the Assabet, however, made night hoarse with their croaking; and we were aroused soon after dawn by the clamorous cawing of a flock of crows, and began the day at an early hour, little refreshed.

Egg Rock is covered with turf and mould, except here and there where the rock protrudes, or a ledge crops out, and an open growth of trees. It is a favorite resort for picnics, and hardly a day goes by in summer without one or more parties making it a scene of bright festivity. We were, however, entirely undisturbed during our stay, except by the report of a gun and the rattle of a scattering charge of shot among the trees somewhat near our heads, a circumstance that was immediately followed by a brief, but somewhat animated, conversation between us and the sportsman; and, upon another occasion, when, on our return from the village, we found a very pretty little girl in the hammock, which, however, was not very much of a disturbance; at least, to us. Frequently, however, during the day we heard the sound of dipping oars, and caught sight of a boat gliding up the Assabet or returning to the village.

Egg Rock is indeed an idyllic spot. The view is a charming pastoral. The Concord, formed by the union of the Sudbury and Assabet, flows away from the end of the rock with rippling current until it shortly disappears beneath a bridge in a causeway. Here and there is a house, and, among others, the Barrett Mansion, which occupies the site of the house the ancestors of the present family lived in at the time of the Concord Fight. The Minute-man and monument are a little distance farther down, and beyond is fold upon fold of green hills and woods. Upon one side, beyond the embankment of the Lowell Railroad, is a blended mass of foliage and houses, which comprise a portion of the village, and on the other the wild and lovely Assabet.

Hawthorne says: "A more lovely stream than the Assabet for a mile above its junction with the Concord has never flowed on earth — nowhere, indeed, except to lave the interior regions of a poet's imagination. . . . It comes flowing softly through the midmost privacy and deepest heart of a wood which whispers it to be quiet; while the stream whispers back again from its sedgy borders, as if river and wood were hushing one another to sleep. Yes; the river sleeps along its course and dreams of the sky and the clustering foliage."

On Wednesday afternoon we rowed up the Assabet. We saw innumerable frogs and a congregation of seven turtles on a board, the very same party, I have no doubt, that Mrs. Goddard, in a sketch of Concord, says she saw while rowing up the Assabet. With heads craned high and motionless in air, like so many pious Moslems, they awaited our approach, and when we were quite near they tumbled into the water one after another, and rapidly kicking hind-legs could be seen vigorously propelling each clumsy creature to the depths below.

On the evening of every Fourth of July a carnival of boats is held on the rivers. One wing of the fleet forms beneath the leafy arches of the Assabet, where the great hemlocks reach over to see their reflections in the black water, and the other on the open Sudbury, and at a given signal the procession, gay with illuminations, moves down the Concord amid a glare of fireworks under the old North Bridge brilliantly adorned with lanterns.

After wandering away from the haunts of men on

The Old Manse

lonely rivers in the midst of nature, where all is apparently plain and simple, we determined to visit the School of Philosophy and listen to the perplexing problems man proposes and discusses. The cosy little building in which the school holds its sessions is new, with interior unfinished and rough, and of itself would surely not awaken any suspicion of distraction, nor, indeed, did the entertaining lecture we heard Mrs. Cheney deliver about early American art. It is, somehow, the fashion to deride the School of Philosophy. Is not learning, however, rather to be congratulated upon the establishment of a school, disjointed it may be, and somewhat fragmentary, where the mystical problems of the mind can be discussed? The problems exist, and though of no immediate practical importance, and perhaps forever insoluble, yet they cannot be dismissed out of sight. The question of preexistence and the primal principles of philosophy and what-not else can surely find no more fitting place for consideration than the Hillside Chapel; where, in an atmosphere of drowsy nature, amiable culture, mature in experience, calmly discusses with frank courtesy the Unthinkable and the Unknown, — the self-same problems that Macaulay declares were discussed and left unsolved by Ionian philosophers three thousand years ago. May the Concord School have better luck!

The conversation that follows each lecture is, however, the real charm of the school, and has given the philosophic enterprise its chief reputation.

The view from Lee's Hill, an inconsiderable elevation that rises behind Egg Rock, is quite extensive, varied, and beautiful. Toward the northwest appears the magnificent extent of the State Prison, like a huge palace —

a palace of misery. The town is below on the right, hemmed by the shining river, which can be seen for some miles sweeping toward the northeast through rich green hills.

The Wayside

There are many points of interest in and about Concord. The tavern wherein Major Pitcairn stirred his famous glass of toddy with a bloody finger, exclaiming, "I will stir the Yankee blood in the same way before night," is still standing, in nearly the same condition as when the Major uttered his bloody threat; and along the road to

Lexington, and in and around the village, are many houses which were standing at the time of the British "occupation." Then, in addition to the Old Manse, there is the Wayside, where Hawthorne resided at the time of his death, the residence of the Hon. E. R. Hoar, and the homes of Emerson, Alcott, and Sanborn. For a more particular description of these, however, and the library, which is quite large and valuable, and the cemeteries and other places and matters of interest, I would refer any one desirous of further information to Bartlett's Concord Guide-book, which is a very interesting, as well as useful, contribution to the literature of the town. The view of the Old Manse given herein is from the rear, or river, side.

CHAPTER III.

CONCORD. — NEWBURYPORT.

WE broke camp on Egg Rock Thursday morning, and about ten o'clock renewed our voyage. After passing the stone bridge which spans the Concord just below the junction of the rivers, we were caught in a shower that had been impending, and on account of which we had delayed our departure. A brief pull, however, brought us to the old North Bridge, where we made fast, and for several hours found shelter upon the historic structure. The bridge itself is so old-fashioned, yet artistic, and the approach on the Concord side through the avenue of hemlocks so beautiful, that the spot would be attractive, even apart from the monuments and historical associations that cluster about it. The Minute-man on the left bank, the monument on the right, and the quaint bridge, contrast strangely with the rural scenes around; while the Old Manse near by, on one side, and elegant houses on the other, complete the bewilderment, I might almost say enchantment, of the place. There is, too, a touch of pathos in the inscription, "Graves of British Soldiers," on a granite ledge set in the stone wall between the hemlocks near the bridge. Two rude stones, peering just above the ground within a scant enclosure, which mark their resting-place, tell a dumb story of pain and woe long past. How easy to call up the scene of conflict! On the south bank the company of red-coated soldiers idling on guard; upon the other the Provincials coming down the road, and then both sides forming for what might be a collision, the British stolid and disposed to sneer at their foemen, the Americans anxious, and

Old North Bridge

eager, and nervous, it may be, still bravely approaching the crisis. Then came a stray bullet from the Britons, followed by a volley that killed Davis and Hosmer, and then the fire of the Americans, after which an indiscriminate loading and firing until the British retired to the town, leaving the two dead, who were buried where they fell.

It was one o'clock when we ventured to embark again, between the stray drops of rain. In a few minutes we passed under the third and last stone bridge at Concord, and soon lost sight of the Minute-man, and in a brief while were again on an aboriginal river. Either the old truism about the inappreciable descent of the Concord River is untrue, or the rains had unduly swollen the volume of water; for the current was, for the most part, quite rapid, and with the help of the oars we swiftly passed along close to one bank or the other, around many a pretty winding turn. I am inclined to think, however, that the current story about a bridge that was blown from its abutments and floated up river, in reality belongs to the Sudbury, which is, in truth, the slowest and laziest river under the sun, and near Concord is often called the Concord.

After a row of nearly three hours, which included a long halt under some trees to escape a shower, as we were pulling along a wide marsh around a sharp bend just within the border-line of the town of Bedford, we espied, at the head of a long reach on the left bank, at the edge of a piece of woods at the foot of a hill, a deserted shanty. The rain — Jupiter Pluvius appeared to be in ascendency all the week — was pouring down quite hard, so we made fast by the shanty, and sought shelter in it. After a while, the rain ceased, and we rowed up river half a mile or more, and after much difficulty in effecting a landing on the marshy shore, renewed our supply of provisions at a farm-house, and returned, besides, with a boatload of dry hay, which contained a great deal of sweet-fern, and made an aromatic couch, full of slumber. Bow here proved an accomplished cook by making an excellent custard, in a very few minutes. He gave solemn assurance that the result was not an accident. We found the name Bull cut in one of the boards of the shanty, and we afterwards ascertained that a man named Bull, from Concord, had lived in the shanty an entire winter, after the manner of Thoreau at Walden Pond. Whatever the comfort of a structure entirely of boards, about ten by eight, and just high enough to stand in, with one small window, and a door, and a hole for a stovepipe, and a sand floor, in winter, we found it very comfortable during our stay, save when a sudden shower in the morning let in an unneeded quantity of water through the leaky roof. Whether Mr. Bull succeeded in reducing his expenses to eight dollars and seventy-six cents for a year, a feat achieved by Thoreau at Walden Pond, I know not; but our thanks, at least, are certainly due him for the use of his building.

We pulled down river Friday afternoon. The reach below the shanty is one of the longest, if not the longest, on the river. Rough woods lined the shore on the left side beyond marshy meadows, while at intervals farm-houses and cultivated fields appeared on the right. After a while the houses and spires of Billerica loomed up on the right bank. Rowing by the abutments of a lost bridge, we made fast just above the middle bridge, the road from which leads direct to the village. Billerica is a very handsome specimen of the more modern New-England village. The view down the valley toward Lowell from the head of the street that leads to the river is exceedingly fine.

After rambling through the village, we returned to the river and pitched our tent under a huge oak at the edge of a grove just above the bridge, hurrying the work to escape a shower impending from the north. The stars were shining brightly all over the sky, except where a castled cloud projected itself slowly upward, shot through with constant, vivid flashes of lightning and accompanied by a loud rumbling of thunder. For an hour or more the shadow of the cloud hung above us, and then edged away to the north, a rainless portent.

The next morning we were early on our way. On the left and lower side of a bridge we pulled under, in the course of the morning row, — I think it was here, although it may have been below the Carlisle-Bedford bridge, — is an old weather-stained house, with barn and outbuildings to match, which rivals in quaint, antique grace the Old Manse at Concord.

Above and below the bridge were innumerable lilies, which bloomed almost continually along the river, only in some places in almost tropical profusion. As we were pulling along at the edge of the lily-pads, Stroke plucked a handsome bud, which in a moment broke into full bloom in his hand. The current below the bridge runs quite swiftly at times over several slight descents. By and by we passed a number of rocks strewn about the channel, and entered the pond above the dam at North Billerica.

Bridge at North Billerica

The oarsman off duty while trolling across the pond succeeded in catching a rock that weighed several tons, and two small pickerel. The dam of the Talbot Mills is easily passed by keeping in the sluice-way on the right to the road. Then, after a short carry across the road into the mill-yard, you can let your boat over a stone embankment into the river.

We hauled to shore on a perfect sand beach on the right, about two miles below North Billerica, and in the woods beyond found a lively brook of remarkably cold water. At three we started for Lowell and at the edge of the city, after passing under three or four bridges, found our way obstructed by a dam. The river-bed below the dam was completely dry. A canal leads off to the left. Following the canal at first and then turning to the end of the dam, we made a portage over the embankment and put the boat into the canal below the gate. We then had good sailing for about a third of a mile, although we were occasionally obliged to lie down in the boat to escape hitting some of the bridges which crossed the canal. We took the boat out at the end of the canal and made a portage of about three hundred feet through the yard of a mill on the right, and, launching the boat down a steep bank, we were soon pulling across another pond, and quickly came to another dam. The second dam can quite easily be passed to the right, though we found no difficulty, on account of the low water, in getting over the middle of it, and we were soon pulling over another pond, to our great discouragement. We were now in the city and houses lined the hills on both sides of the pond. At the end of the pond on the left was a huge brick mill, and over a high dam we could see the water curling and hear it plunging below. A carry is feasible around a low building to the right of the dam. We approached the dam itself, however, at a corner of the building, and found just space enough, where the water was only trickling over the flash-boards, to pull the boat up and slide her over the dam, and amid the thundering roar of the water, which loudly resounds when one is near below it, we launched her below the fall. Then, after a few strokes, we entered a sort of canal, and shooting across a deep revolving whirlpool, formed by the inrushing waste water from the Merrimac canal, we were borne on the surging current under Merrimac-street bridge into the Merrimac.

We had been two hours in getting by the three dams. No good landing-place appeared near, however, so Stroke turned the boat about and put her, stern foremost, through Hunt's Falls, on the Lowell side. The waves leaped menacingly above the stern, and the spray flew around in little showers for a moment or two; but the swift motion was a very agreeable sensation after the slow work over dams and ponds. The row of brick mills which extends along the south shore of the Merrimac until the view is intercepted by a bend, presents a massive and imposing frontage on the river. We drew to shore at the foot of the rapid, and spent the night in the City of Spindles.

On the morrow we found that the channel over which we had swiftly floated the night before was completely dry. The river had, indeed, on account of the shutting off of the water, almost entirely disappeared. We passed through a very narrow channel at first, and then keeping to the left of an island just below, dropped down the river a few miles, and in the evening encamped on the left bank, about a mile above Lawrence.

Lawrence is nine miles below Lowell, and the river the entire distance is wide, and the banks woody and picturesque. A large island lies nearer the left shore, about half way between the two places, and immediately below, on the left, are some handsome stretches of open country, marked here and there by farm-houses and, farther down, finely wooded hills. The river, quite deep, with little current, is a favorite cruising ground for many small yachts, which add life to the water. The Merrimac is indeed a famous river for boating. As we sat under our tent, in the moonlit evening, we saw many boats go by, and the music of sacred songs was wafted across the water from far and near.

At daybreak on Monday morning we climbed to the top of the hill which rose from the river where we were encamped, and had a magnificent view of the sunrise. Below was Lawrence, still and sleeping, — I had almost said lazy, — to the south were Andover and West Andover on a ridge of hills, while the course of the river could be traced westward by the mists which rolled above it. It is a fine location for a farm, and the milk we obtained at the house which crowns the summit of the hill was quite as good as the view. After a breakfast of the tenderest of sirloin, and the sweetest roasted potatoes, and the most delicious coffee, — I speak wholly with reference to the taste, and not at all to the actual quality of the articles, — we rowed along shore and soon came to the head of the broad canal on the left of the river, which supplies the motive power to the mills of Lawrence.

The water glides swiftly into the canal, and rushes furiously under the bridge. Boats have been swept under, and care must be exercised in approaching it. The lockman opened the gate at one side of the bridge in a few minutes, and we pulled into the canal below, where the water pours along full of little whirlpools, but entirely safe. The current is very swift at first, and carried us along very rapidly past the mills on one side, where the machinery made incessant roar, and the long lines of brick houses on the other. We had to lie down in the bottom of the boat to pass some of the bridges. After a very novel and agreeable voyage of about half a mile, perhaps, we came to the end of the canal, where we were let down thirty-two feet through three locks, in about twenty minutes, into the river below. The sensation, as you sit in the boat in a lock and feel the water sinking beneath you, induces a slight sense of horror, to say the least. There is no charge for locking.

The current is very swift below Lawrence, but the

banks are not nearly so pretty as above. About four miles below Lawrence is an island, and immediately below the island is a short stretch of rapids. The best channel, marked by buoys, is used by small steamers; but I should think they would have a hard time in getting through.

We turned the boat about and went through stern foremost, enjoying that most delightful of sensations, the motion of rushing water. The river makes a sharp bend below the fall, and along the lower side of the bend is another rapid. The swift water carried us along near the shore past the steamer Kittie Boynton, moored alongside the bank. Below the rapid, the current continues quite strong in the middle of the river, between lines of buoys, nearly to the end of the reach, where, after rounding a bend, we saw the city of Haverhill. We pulled up at a wharf under the passenger bridge at eleven o'clock, having made the nine miles from Lawrence in two hours and a half. Here, to our surprise, we were informed that the tide was just beginning to go out; so, after only a few minutes' delay, we went along with it.

Pulling by Groveland, about two miles below Haverhill, we kept on for about a mile, when we pulled up on the beach and had the last of the dinners of the trip, which somehow, in spite of the crude cookery, were always literally devoured with a relish. Then keeping on down river, with wind and tide and current in our favor, we soon came in sight of West Newbury, and for a time wondered what was the course of the river, as the hills seemed to enclose it on every side. The river turned northward, however, and soon we were pulling through an interminable reach, where a strong head wind made very toilsome the incessant efforts of the weary oarsmen, and was, I fear, the occasion of some pious ejaculations. Then Merrimacport appeared on the right bank. Several unpainted, weather-stained, old-fashioned houses give the village a quaint and pleasing aspect.

After pulling through two or three quite long reaches, Amesbury appeared before us, and rounding a long cape of sand heaps that projected from the right bank just below Laurel Hill, formerly the summer residence of the English Minister Thornton, a slight elevation, which, nevertheless, commands one of the loveliest views in New England, we met the incoming tide and another head wind. Pulling diagonally down river past the rocky north shore, by a very handsome edifice of brick and stone, we directed our course toward the channel on the lower side of an island, on which is the Spofford residence. Rowing under the old chain bridge, which in part connects Salisbury with Newburyport, and forms a quaint contrast with the more modern structure over the channel on the north side of the island, we crept along close to shore, and were, I believe, an hour and a half in going a mile and a half to Shaw's Wharf, where our voyage ended.

We had been eleven days on the three rivers, and had made a distance of about one hundred miles in all.

The Sudbury, from Southville to Saxonville, cannot be navigated without a great deal of toil and trouble, and the Merrimac is too wide to furnish the peculiar pleasure which comes from following the continuous windings of a small stream; but the Sudbury, from Stone's Bridge at Saxonville to Concord, and the Concord thence to North Billerica, a distance of nearly fifty miles in all, is free from any difficulty; and each stream, narrow, deep, and, generally, sluggish, is a delightful river to descend. I commend the nameless graces of each to all who love to follow the Unknown River.

I may add that Saxonville is the terminus of a branch of the Boston and Albany Railroad, and the station of the Lowell Railroad at North Billerica is only a few minutes' walk from the mills.

PRACTICAL SUGGESTIONS.

I ought perhaps to say, by way of advice to any one who has a desire to take a boating trip, that almost any boat is suitable for the purpose, provided it is light and portable.

In the absence of any choice, however, I would recommend, especially for two persons, an eleven-foot skiff, and spruce oars seven and one-half feet long.

A back should be fitted to the stern seat of the boat, as it adds greatly to the comfort and ease of the oarsman off duty.

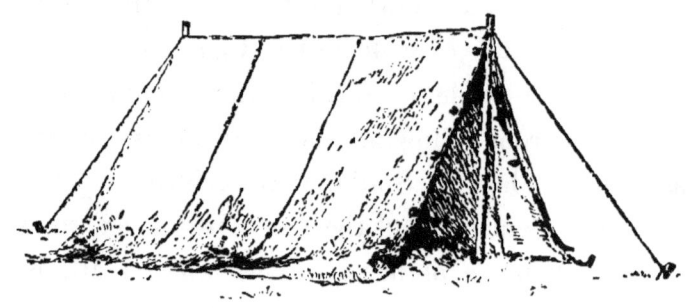

Three oars should be taken in preference to a pair alone.

A painter of extra length should be provided, and a long stern rope may be very useful at times in rapids.

A tent, such as the one I have used, which has proved very serviceable, may easily be made as follows. The main canvas is about sixteen feet long and seven wide. This is stretched over a ridge-pole and fastened to the ground by pegs, three on each side, attached to double holes in the canvas about a foot and a half from the edge, thus leaving a projecting flap when the tent is up. At the rear of the tent a triangular piece of canvas may be sewed to one half of the main piece, and can then be buttoned on the other side and fastened close to the ground by four or five pegs. For the front of the tent, instead of using canvas or leaving it entirely open, I have used two large pieces of mosquito-netting. By pinning these to the edge of the tent and allowing them to fall in folds on the ground, one is protected against mosquitoes and other plagues o' the night, while the projecting flaps, weighted, with the oars, for instance, keep them out at the sides. Cotton drilling, which comes two feet four and a half inches in width, and sells at eight to ten cents per yard, is sufficiently stout, and twenty-five yards is enough for the main and rear pieces.

Duck, which is considerably heavier and a little more durable, is of the same width, and costs from twelve to seventeen cents per yard.

I have always cut ridge-pole and supports at the beginning of a trip and carried them along to the end. I think, however, that it might be well to prepare two light supports of seasoned wood sharpened at the lower ends and covered with an iron ferrule, with holes in the top, through which a cord could be passed and knotted on either side of each support to keep it from slipping. The cord should then be fastened at each end to a peg which is to be driven into the ground at a suitable distance from the bottom of the support. Five feet and eight inches is sufficiently high for the supports.

It usually took us not over ten minutes to pitch our tent, using supports and ridge-pole of green wood; but with the improvements I have suggested it would take

still less time and the tent would be more trim and secure, though our tent always stood up in all sorts of weather and never leaked.

Of course one can readily dispense with a tent altogether and stop at hotels in the villages. If, however, one stops at hotels he may nevertheless enjoy a bit of camp life by taking along cooking utensils and supplies. All that is necessary of the former are coffee-pot, tea-pot, a frying-pan (preferably the Acme), sauce-pan, tin cups, tin plates, knives, forks, and spoons. Other necessary adjuncts to camping are a hatchet and candlestick. As for supplies, tastes differ; but almost everything desired, including fresh meat ordinarily, can be obtained at villages along the rivers. Canned roast beef and baked beans are, however, always good to start with and keep in the larder, and campers-out now generally agree that tea, perhaps English breakfast tea, is fully as much a necessity as coffee.

In camping, a thick comforter is, I think, the best kind of a blanket. It is necessary to have a rubber blanket also, an overcoat, preferably an old one; and a rubber coat is very useful under any circumstance.

A canvas bag is very convenient to keep the tent in and various odds and ends, and a box should be made with a cover for cooking utensils and supplies.

These suggestions may be useful in some respects, perhaps, to many who already have found pleasure and health in the ever new and delightful experiences of a boating trip, and they will, I hope, be still more serviceable to those to whom such a trip would be an entire novelty.

AN AUTUMN CRUISE

ON

THE HOUSATONIC

FROM

PITTSFIELD TO THE SOUND.

CHAPTER I.

PITTSFIELD. — LEE.

A RIVER is a musical poem. Like the strains of an orchestra its various streams unite and pour forward in rhythmic melody. Then, too, a river like a fine epic is well adorned, having for its constant themes woods and hills and mountains, a mill or a village, farm-houses and bridges, and a genuine atmosphere overhead. An epic is likely, however, to grow tiresome; a river, never. You read a poem; you enjoy a river.

The Housatonic River, the finest of poems, is the chief ornament of Berkshire County, the finest of prose.

The west branch of the Housatonic rises among the Hoosac Mountains of northwestern Massachusetts, a section of the State which has not inaptly been called the Switzerland of America. The principal source of the west branch is in the town of Lanesborough. Lake Pontoosuc, a broad and beautiful sheet of water, dotted with two islands in the middle, may be considered, however, the actual head from which the stream flows south to Pittsfield. The principal source of the east branch is in Hinsdale, though a multitude of small streams join above Dalton, and their commingling waters flow westward along the line of the Boston and Albany Railroad to unite with the west branch just below Pittsfield. The river after the union of the two branches flows in a generally southerly direction through western Massachusetts and western Connecticut for about one hundred and fifty miles to Long Island Sound. It derives its name from the Housatonic tribe of Indians, which formerly inhabited its banks. I have somewhere read that Housatonic signified in the Indian tongue, "Over the mountains;" but I should think a more correct interpretation might be "Among the mountains."

I had an appointment to meet a friend at Pittsfield toward the latter part of September for the purpose of taking a row down the Housatonic — to enjoy a poem without reading. The skiff which was to embody the movement, the same one I had used in a voyage down the Sudbury, Concord, and Merrimac, was sent from Boston to Pittsfield about the middle of September by the American Express Company. The expressage was three dollars and ninety cents, double the ordinary rate. The fare from Boston is three dollars and forty cents.

Pittsfield, the shire town of the county, settled in 1752, and named after William Pitt, the great English commoner, has a population of about twelve thousand. It is situated in the triangular space formed within the two branches of the river. The Boston and Albany Railroad intersects the town like the bar of an A, the branches of the river representing the prolongations of

THE HOUSATONIC RIVER.

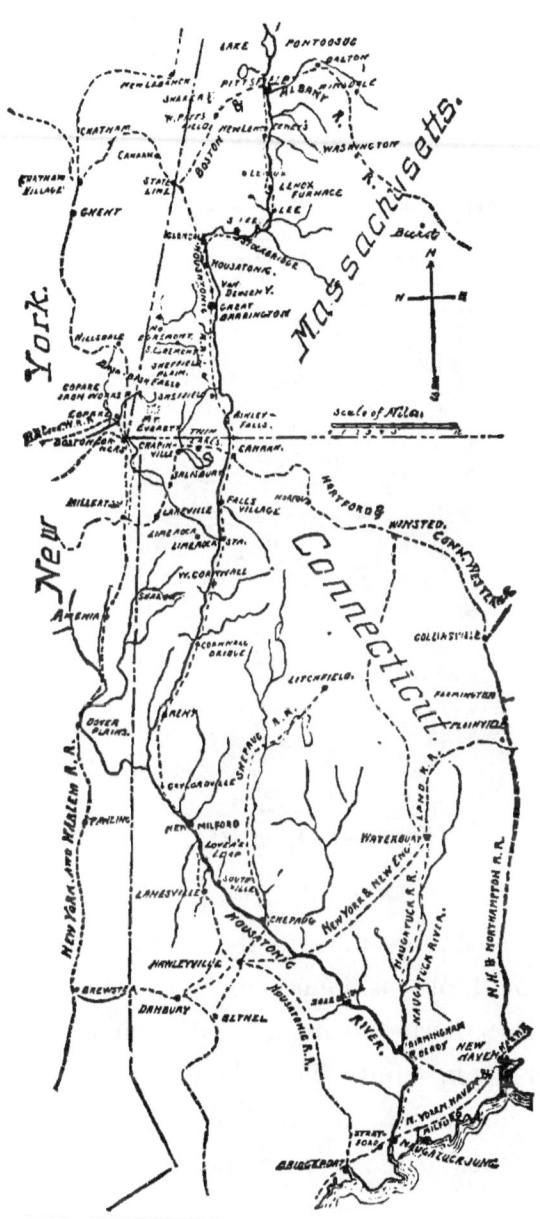

the letter. From a square about the middle of the town four streets radiate toward each point of the compass, called respectively North, South, East, and West Streets. On the north side of the square is the old Town Hall, while

Hawthorne's Writing Desk

opposite is a very handsome library of unique and artistic design. In the Athenæum in the upper part of the library is a small, old-fashioned, upright mahogany desk upon which Hawthorne wrote The Blithedale Romance, The Wonder-Book, and The House of the Seven Gables, while he lived in the little old red house on the north side of Stockbridge Bowl in Lenox.

After dining at the American House, as the friend who was to accompany me on the river was busily engaged in concocting a brief, or some such contrivance, it was agreed that I should take the boat alone to Lenox Station, where he was to join me on the arrival of the five o'clock train from Pittsfield, and we were then to go on to Lee together. I proceeded to the office of the express company, and was there subjected to a petty annoyance without rhyme and with little reason. The agent declined to deliver the boat at the river at South-street bridge on the ground that it was beyond the schoolhouse, which he affirmed was the limit of delivery. It was beyond, but only a few rods, and it seemed as if there might be a slight concession to the exigency of the case; but no, the *ipse dixit* of the agent was as decisive as the fulmination of a Roman emperor. It behooved me, therefore, to find another place to launch the craft, and I soon ascertained that the west branch was navigable below Pomeroy's lower woolen-mill. Here, however, another difficulty arose. The aforesaid agent declined to deliver the boat until after five o'clock, so that it finally became necessary to procure a team at additional expense and a great deal of additional trouble.

The teamster and I put the boat in the river below the last building of the mill, which is on West Housatonic Street. It would be, however, an easy matter to get over the dams of both woolen-mills. The boat had been in ordinary several weeks, and the instant it touched the water, to use the familiar expression, leaked like a sieve. By this time several operatives from the mill had gathered

Pomeroy's lower Mill Pittsfield.

around, and we lifted the boat on a walk, turned her over, and I was engaged an hour or more in caulking the widely distended seams, an operation in which one or another of the constantly relayed group of interested observers took a hand. It is always advisable to have a little oakum and oil-of-tar in boating. I had neither. I must admit, however, and had supposed there could be no possible occasion for anything of the sort, as the boat had been both caulked and painted in anticipation of the trip. We used cotton batting, the only thing available, which proved quite serviceable, though I suspect that the soaking in the water was the most effective remedy. I had invited any one of my co-laborers who felt so disposed to join me as far as Lenox Station, and when the boat was ready for its final launch a volunteer appeared, arrayed in his Sunday best.

We put the boat in once more and started on the voyage about three o'clock. The stream below the mill is about thirty feet wide, and winds very pleasantly in a small, narrow valley of its own. We soon came to a brand new wire fence which extended directly across our path and looked like a very troublesome obstacle, as the wires were full of sharp projections. Drifting to it, however, stern foremost, my passenger lifted the lowest strand over his head, I carried the thorny burden precariously over my own, and we passed under without a scratch. Just above South-street bridge we ran against a log boomed across the stream. We passed close to the west bank under the west end of the log by depressing the boat nearly to the gunwale in the water. I do not believe that the boat displaced quite so much water again during the trip. Pulling under the old wooden bridge immediately below, we rowed around a bend and bunted against another log lying across the stream. My companion in assisting to lift the boat over the east end lost his footing on the mossy bank, and slid into the water considerably above his knees, amid expressions of great disgust. We quickly got the boat over, however, and started on and soon came to another obstruction in the shape of a plank walk. We found just room enough, however, to pass under the east end with ease.

The river had been continually rapid, and we went swiftly forward, now past a clump of woods and now along open meadows with both banks and hillsides near at hand. The water, discolored by the refuse of the mills above, and darkened still more by dense, threatening clouds overhead, flowed with peculiar shady effects over a grassy bed in shallow places, though the bottom could not be seen at all in the deeper pools. There was always sufficient water, however, and after we got below the junction of the east branch, a stream about the same size and consistency as the other, we had an abundance. I allude to the state of the water, as the trip had been delayed on account of a fear that we would not have sufficient water to get along at all, as the season had been remarkably dry. I have little hesitation, however, in saying that the river from Pittsfield to Falls Village is navigable in a flat-bottomed boat at all times; and that one can indeed get along below Falls Village, too, although the greater the volume of water below that point the greater the pleasure of a trip.

The river soon wound under another bridge and then writhed in extraordinary fashion in quite an extensive intervale. We loitered along its windings, the swift current beguiling us into thinking that we were making great progress and would easily reach Lenox Station by five o'clock. Greylock drifted to and fro across the rear of the valley in the distance to the north. Perhaps, however, it was the winding river that drifted to and fro. I know not how it may have been: the effect was the same, and even now in memory I see a blue mountain of vaguely beautiful outline, solemnly moving from side to side across a valley landscape, shadowily picturesque.

The clouds, however, threatened rain every moment, and the rising wind, blowing fresh as if from the ocean, added stimulus to our constant apprehension of an immediate downpour. It did not come, however, but the darkness above only served to bestow on all the valley an intense, deep, sombre green. No house was in sight, and all was silence. The river was as variable in its course as the wind is usually supposed to be, and sometimes, assuming that the wind was steadfast, we had the breeze at our back, frequently on one side or the other, and occasionally in our faces. After a while I resigned the oars to my companion, who had long been itching to row. He exerted his muscle with terrific force, and, as the boat was light, and easy rowing, and quickly turned, he produced some startling aberrations from the ordinary line of our progress. His knees were the occasion of a great deal of trouble. Having once got the stroke well past those troublesome projections, however, he was all right for the rest of it. Taking one quite desperate stroke, however, after the usual interruption at the knees, there was a loud crack and the rowing-seat, which was thin and springy, broke into a half-dozen pieces and let the oarsman down to the bottom of the boat with a great shock. Luckily we had with us a stray board which we had used as a rest to keep our feet out of the water which poured into the boat in spite of the cotton batting, and this was made to answer for a rowing-seat, while thereafter we bailed oftener than ever.

And now the river had come to a woody mountain on the east side of the valley, and began a game of tag with the high and mighty dignitary. It ran up to the mountain, and then edged away in the devious ways known only to a river, and then again, after approaching the immovable and dignified mountain, bounded away over the meadows. After a while we heard a train whistling ahead, and, as it was past five o'clock, we concluded we were not far from Lenox Station. We had not once caught sight of the railroad, however. Pulling rapidly on we came to a bridge, the fifth from Pittsfield, I think, and below on the west bank was a large house. Inquiring of a boy where we were, he said at Dewey's Station, which is only three miles below Pittsfield. The boy — he was not an encouraging youth at all — gave a very disheartening account of the long distance still before us to Lenox Station; but both my companion and myself, voting him an ill-omened prophet, decided that there was nothing else to be done but keep on.

The river from Dewey's goes with an evener current, and renewed the game of tag with a range of mountains which begins just below. Soon after starting, the clouds, which mercifully for us had not dispensed rain, not even a drop, broke into fleecy mists and drifted away, tinged with a deep red glow by the setting sun. After a while we found ourselves on a dark river in a very dark landscape. And now my companion proved to be a companion indeed. Malachi was an optimist. He assured me every few strokes that it could not be far to Lenox now, and in truth I often gave him the same assurance in return. We were once startled nearly out of our wits by the voice of a man on a bank fishing. We had not perceived him at all when he broke the deep, black solitude by asking us if we could assist him to splice the main brace. We explained that we were not sailors, only oarsmen. In vain I endeavored to ascertain whether we were in the pond opposite Lenox Station, but I could not tell when we passed through it, nor see the station, though we passed within fifty yards of it, and Malachi was as ignorant as myself. We finally pulled under a bridge, and, just below, the bow of the boat grated harshly on the gravel at the edge of a stone dam. Entirely unfamiliar with the locality, and, as we had apparently not passed through any pond, thinking that we had not yet arrived at Lenox, we nevertheless moored the boat, as the channel below the dam was dry. As a matter of fact, the dépôt of Lenox Station was at the end of the bridge we had just passed, but having no suspicion of it, and still encouraged by the optimism of my friend Malachi, whose tendency, as well as my own, was forward, we walked down the track with alternations of doubt and conviction, a mile to Lenox Furnace; and then, after sending a telegram to my intended fellow-voyager who had gone on to Lee, we retraced our steps to Lenox Station, where, upon the departure of the nine-o'clock train that carried Malachi back to Pittsfield, I took the stage to Lenox, distant two and one-half miles, and found shelter, which I had at one time seriously despaired of obtaining, at Curtis's Hotel. In the office I gazed with a present sympathy upon an allegorical picture which graced one of the walls: "The Voyage of Life — Old Age." On the hearth the embers of the fire sent a thrill of warmth through me, for the night air was cold, and supper, a ten o'clock one, — the table is excellent, — soon sent another of a different and better kind. The hotel is quite a fashionable resort and performs its share in what Mr. James, in his note about Hawthorne (a very poetic strain of criticism, not in the least inconclusive), calls the lionization of Lenox. Numerous odds and ends of antique bric-à-brac are scattered over the house. The rage for that sort of thing may indeed be said to reach high-water mark in Curtis's large, and, in the way indicated, old-fashioned and comfortable hostelry.

I took the early coach the following morning, to meet my fellow-voyager on the arrival of the early train at the station. The regular stage-driver is also, strange to say, the station-agent, a remarkable union of callings, it seems to me. Another driver, however, took his place, who, as it turned out, had no key to the station wherein our oars and baggage had been locked up the night before, and so we had to wait nearly an hour for the arrival of the double-headed functionary before we could get our stuff and go on. How odd the scene around looked by the garish light of day! There was the pond, or, rather, a narrow channel through the middle of a wide expanse of mud, and the bridge, and the river, all as plain as need be!

We found the gate at the head of the sluice-way at the east end of the dam raised so we could pass under; otherwise it would have been necessary to carry over on the east side, as it is not advisable, under any circumstances, I should think, to try the river below the dam. Following the canal, we soon came to another dam. Taking the boat out below the gate-way, we had a very short carry around the lower side of the mill to the river. The mill belongs to the Smith Paper Company, and is known as the Pleasant Valley Mill. Paper is made here one hundred inches wide, on the largest machine in the country.

Lenox Furnace.

Pulling on down stream, we soon came in sight of a bridge, above which rose, just beyond on the west bank, the square tower, surmounted by three brick chimneys, of an iron furnace, which sometime apparently impressed the name Lenox Furnace on the small settlement thereabout. The dam is just below the bridge. If water is pouring over the dam, the best way to get around is to go to the west shore, and carry around the grist-mill, putting in under the barrel-flume below. The water was so low that we let the boat down over the middle of the dam. We pulled by the furnace, which has an air of ancient greatness gone to rack and ruin, and in a few minutes came to another dam of the Smith Paper Company. We carried two or three rods, and put in the sluice-way on the east side of the dam, and thence floated down to the mill, where we carried the boat around the mill on a wheelbarrow, and put in the tail-race just below. A high bank made it awkward to launch the boat, and the stern dipped some water. After bailing, several hundred lucky-bugs that had been scooped in remained and beat an incessant and multitudinous tattoo. The water ran swiftly in the race, and we soon emerged into the river. Ere long we came to an island, and attempting to get by got aground, and had to go back and take the west side, where is an abundance of swift water. Immediately below, the river spread out over a gravelly bed, and we had very hard work to push over. The banks are quite picturesque here, especially just above and below an old wooden bridge. A range of mountains which borders the valley on the east adds fine emphasis to the scene. All admiration of scenery, however, was soon stopped by another dam, which furnishes motive power to the Columbia Mills. If the water is high, the best way to get by is to pull over the embankment on the west side. We made a carry on the east side with a wheelbarrow. Then a short pull over a pond-like stretch of water, past a row of houses on the east side in the village of Lee, brought us to the dam of the Eagle Mills. If the water is high, it is better to carry over on the west bank. We had a hard tug of it on the east side, taking out just above the mill, and lugging the boat across the road before we could put in. Immediately below is the dam of the Housatonic Mill. Here it is necessary to put in the sluice-way on the east side. We left our boat at the bridge just above the mill, which is very nearly the centre of the village.

CHAPTER II.

LEE. — GREAT BARRINGTON.

LEE is an energetic and thriving village, having a much more business-like appearance than other towns along the river. The most striking feature of natural beauty is Fern Cliff, a rugged ledge of granite, crowned, however, with graceful trees, that frowns upon the town just back of the principal street. We remained at Lee two days, and one afternoon attended the annual meeting of the Fern Cliff Association, a society which has for its object the improvement of the streets of the village, and chiefly attending to sidewalks and crossings, and setting out shade-trees and shrubbery. The meeting was held on Fern Cliff, which commands a very fine view of the houses of the village below, and the river and Berkshire Hills. A very eloquent address was delivered by the Rev. Washington Gladden, on The Use of the Beautiful. The accomplished orator spoke in the open air, in the midst of a scene of beauty that was indeed an omnipresent commentary on his theme. There is an association of the same character at Stockbridge called the Laurel Hill Society, from an elevation near by, which has wrought a marvel in the appearance of that beautiful place, and keeps it in a marvelously fine condition. It is to be hoped, indeed, that a society having the same object will spring up in every village throughout the land.

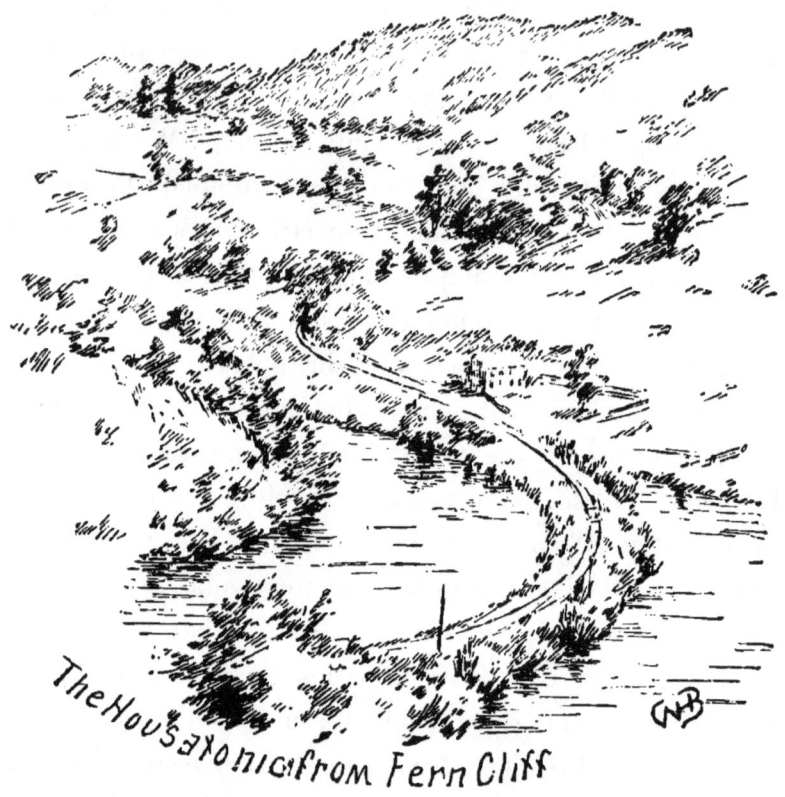

The Housatonic from Fern Cliff

The customary and favorite drive from Lee is to Lenox, distant about three miles. The distinguishing characteristic of Nahant is brown paint, Newport affects the veranda, and Saratoga the broad piazza; but life at Lenox is incomplete unless one lives in a house sided with shingles. There is the old-fashioned colonial mansion, too, and the more modern box, and a great variety of styles besides. Formerly the county seat, the old Court House and town buildings impart to the village an exaggerated idea of past importance. It overflows with fashionable life through a long season. There is also, withal, a distinctive literary flavor about the town. Hawthorne, Beecher, Holmes, Mrs. Kemble, Miss Sedgwick, Miss Cushman, have all lived there at times; while Longfellow, James, and Melville have dwelt in the valley near at hand. It has, however, as its crowning glory, a constant vision of a broad landscape of valley and mountain, indescribably blended in beauty. The drive is then, ordinarily, to the top of Bald Head Mountain, which commands a fine prospect of the "brilliant and generous" landscape. The view southward is, in truth, superb. Below, near at hand, is Stockbridge Bowl; beyond, rising above fertile upland and lowland, a rolling plain of field and forest, is Monument Mountain, while a range of the Green Mountains guards the valley on the east, and the Taconic range, which mounts high up in air in the Dome, runs along the western side. Then the drive is along the road that leads near the northerly edge of the Bowl, by Tanglewood, made famous as a residence of Hawthorne. It is a small, red house, with a wing on the west side, which was formerly the east wing. Apart from this change, however, and a few slight alterations within, the house is the same as when it was occupied by Hawthorne. On a glass in one of the windows is still preserved the inscription, cut in the author's own handwriting, "Nath'l Hawthorne, March 21st, 1853." There are open fire-places in two of the rooms, but its chief value as a residence is the beautiful landscapes the windows on the south side of the house frame of the Berkshire Hills.

From Tanglewood a road leads direct to Stockbridge, one of the most beautiful villages in the Housatonic valley; and thence one may return to Lee either by a road over the hills or along the river. This drive is, throughout, in a region of fashion. One is, indeed, almost as likely to meet a four-in-hand as a farmer's wagon. Fine residences are frequent, and everywhere are evidences of careful cultivation.

There is a lonesome drive, however, east of Lee, which is very fine in its way, and in some respects superior to the other. The road leads just north of the village, through a long, steep, woody pass between two mountains to the town of Washington. The original settlers have of late years, though, for the most part, descended into the valley or flown westward, and a foreign population has largely succeeded to the old farms; and now upon the high lands here, remote from city or village, many a son of Erin cultivates his scanty potato patch, grazes his cattle, and views with utmost complacency a noble landscape of tumbling mountains. Then continuing south along the upland to the road from Becket, you turn westward, and from the summit of the mountain, as you prepare to descend, the view is more than simply beautiful: it is grand. The road itself is visible only a short distance as it winds down the side of the mountain, and there is naught else to be seen but a billowy sea of forests, rising and falling in mountain crests until they dash upward in the distant horizon in the misty hights of the lordly Catskills. The striking feature of the scene, due to the singular vantage of the point of view, is the utter absence of anything like civilization, even a cultivated field. You might be among the fastnesses of the Adirondacks or the wilds of Maine, for aught that appears. The road below is winding and steep in places, but from East Lee pretty level and straight to Lee.

On Saturday morning we renewed the voyage. We carried the boat around the west side of the mill and put her in the tail-race just below, and got off at ten o'clock on a swift current of Tiberish yellow. We stopped on the west shore, just below the outlet of the canal, and climbed up the bank, over the refuse of a quarry, to the edge of the excavation which looked like an inverted windowless palace of white marble. It is a singular fact that white marble is frequently used in and about Lee for foundations and walls, seemingly a base prostitution of pure and valuable material. The river is narrow, and winds very pleasantly with a rippling current past the East Lee valley, and then at the mouth of the wider valley which runs between two mountain ranges to Tyringham, pursuing here, for many miles, a westerly course as far as Glendale. The Housatonic is, in truth, a confirmed coquette, constantly flirting with one mountain range or another, and frequently several at the same time.

Our sudden and unexpected appearance was the occasion of stampeding several horses, and quite often an affright to the patient cow who usually turned and clumsily trotted away in a state of mild distraction. We rowed very close to two Alderney bossies, however, who stood with forefeet firmly planted in the water and gazed at us with melancholy surprise in their wide-open, innocent brown eyes, curiosity evidently overcoming their fear. After rowing about an hour, we met two boys coming up stream with an effort, in a light outrigged pair oar, who turned about and accompanied us under the railroad bridge, and thence, across the pond, to the dam at South Lee. We put ashore on the east side, and in a few minutes (twelve in all, I believe), with the help of the boys, had carried in front of the mill of the Hurlbut Paper Company, and after sliding the boat over a stone embankment opposite the middle of the west side of the mill, launched her on the river. Just below the mill we entered a westward sweep calmly curving between bordering trees, and pulled away from a steep, densely wooded mountain slope which rises sheer from the east end, and seemed to grow higher and higher with every stroke. A rock peered out of water here and there, but there was a fair current and the going was very delightful all the way to Stockbridge. Just above the village, we passed under a slender bridge which leads to Icy Glen, half a mile distant on the east side, where ice is said to remain all the year round. At one o'clock we pulled ashore under the west end of the bridge which leads from the station at Stockbridge, to the village.

Stockbridge is a singularly beautiful New England village. It is located on a broad and fertile intervale close to the Housatonic. The principal avenue, which is a little over a mile in length, is nearly straight and nearly one hundred and fifty feet wide in its widest part. It is, of course, well shaded by long rows of trees, and is kept scrupulously clean. The houses beneath the drooping elms are very tasteful, and there hangs about the entire village an air of aristocratic quiet very graceful and becoming. Stockbridge obtains its chief distinction as having been the residence of Jonathan Edwards. The house is still pointed out where he wrote his most famous production, The Freedom of the Will. A monument has been erected to his memory in Stockbridge Street. At the lower end of the street, on a slight elevation, is an uncouth, unhewn stone, perhaps thirty feet high, and upon the base the inscription, "The Ancient Burial Place of the Stockbridge Indians — The Friends of Our Fathers. 1734." There are many beautiful residences in and around the village, among others the summer home of David Dudley Field, the well-known New York lawyer, Henry M. Field, the editor, and Ivison, the book publisher. The towns of Great Barrington and Stockbridge, Lenox and Lee, are all indeed fine tributes on man's part toward the adornment of a remarkably picturesque and beautiful region.

We dined at the Stockbridge House, which, like Curtis's Hotel, abounds in old-fashioned colonial bric-à-brac. Among other furnishings are fine ancient stoves for open wood-fires. One is surmounted by a huge iron dome that embodies a strange conceit of the beautiful in ornamentation.

We got under way again at two o'clock, and greatly

enjoyed the sail along the winding, watery lane below the bridge. The river is very crooked. At one place we approached quite close to a church and the stone tower, inclosing a chime of bells, erected in commemoration of the site where John Sargeant first preached the gospel to the Indians, and presented to the town by Mrs. David Dudley Field, and then shot away, leaving it behind forever, as we supposed. The river, however, after wandering a long way eastward, returned again almost to the base of the tower, I was about to say, and the tower disappeared and came into view several times thereafter. Below we passed around the ox-bow. The banks were frequently lined with willows, and were often dense with masses of creeping vines. We pulled by a very cosy landing on the east side, where were moored three boats of a high and dainty aspect. I should think, indeed, that there would be more boating here, as the stream is wide, the current slow, and the banks and all the scenery remarkably fine. The river is superior on some accounts to the Concord at Concord, simply lacking boating cultivation. It flows slowly to Glendale, where there is a dam and mill. We bunted the bow of the boat against a corner of the bulkhead on the west side, directly in front of the tower of the mill, and procuring a wheelbarrow wheeled the boat around. It was only seven minutes from the time we touched the bulkhead before we were again under way in the swift current below the mill. In a few minutes the river makes an exceedingly acute bend, which the railroad follows on the east bank. At the end of the bend is a high dam with a red mill on the west bank below. We landed at the easterly end of the dam and made the carry over it in about twelve minutes. The

South Glendale

channel below is quite wide and shallow, and is best navigable on the east side. Just below the mill, however, the various streams unite and pour through a narrow channel, in which are two large rocks set diagonally in the current a little way apart. The oarsman intended to go near the west shore; but the current proved too strong and swept us down toward the rocks with great force and we passed between them with a rush, and, luckily, without touching. The river below is shallow and rocky. It is not dangerous, but very bothersome. We bumped on rocks, and every once in a while hitting some obstruction, let the boat swing around, so that we sometimes went bow on, though most of the time, and such was our intention, stern foremost. The Housatonic Railroad crosses the river on a bridge just above the end of the shallows. The stretch of rapids is a short half-mile in length, though a very long one indeed it seemed in reality. Not far below the end of the shallows is a fall, safe to run at almost any stage of water. We plunged through stern foremost in fine style, and then passed between the fragmentary ends of a ruined dam by some miserably old and wretched abandoned buildings on the east bank, going at a lively pace in swift water. Shortly below, — I think it was here; — the river divides into several channels, and we wandered a long time through one, a delightful, narrow, leaf-embowered waterpath, where the current ran deep and swift through many a circuitous crook before finding its way to the main stream again.

The river rounds the northerly end of Monument Mountain and then half way along its westerly side, until stopped at the dam of the Monument Mills, at Housatonic. The mountain, covered with a scraggy growth of trees, rises precipitously from the water. Near the summit are rugged façades of rough granite. The summit, which is in the middle of the valley, commands a wide, circular view of great beauty. The elevation derives its name from a tradition that an Indian maiden, blighted in love and unable to overcome her passion, sought relief and eternity by jumping from one of the cliffs. Her body was interred where it was found, and above her grave was built up "a cone of small, loose stones." Every visitor thereafter, even when all her dusky compatriots had vanished from the scene, added, as in duty bound, a stone to the pile, which at length became a monument of imposing dimensions. A veritable iconoclast, however, put an end to the venerable custom a long time ago, by scattering the pile to discover what was beneath, and, most proper retribution, found nothing for his trouble. The mountain itself, which had always within memory been called Monument Mountain, is now, indeed, the single eternal memorial of her sad fate.

The story is very happily embalmed in verse by Bryant.

Hawthorne compares Monument Mountain, clad in rich and diversified autumnal foliage, to a huge, headless sphinx wrapped in a Persian shawl.

We landed by a clump of willows on the west shore, and at the village store found a team, upon which we were carried, with the boat, across the bridge and around the end of Cone's Mill, where, after a delay of only twenty minutes in all, we put in the tail-race and swiftly floated into the pond above Cone's new mill, which is about half a mile below the other. We landed at the west end of the dam, and without much trouble hauled the boat over a gravel embankment, and after sliding her down the lower side, started on. Only a slender stream of water was pouring over the dam, and we found the channel below very shallow in several places; and just above a wire fence we had to take the boat out and lower her by means of a cord at the bow and another at the stern, into the end of the tail-race. The mill comprises two large buildings of brick, with stone trimmings, and it is altogether the handsomest mill structure on the Housatonic. I should think all the dams at Housatonic might be carried by on the west side; but they are so near together, and the carries would be, the first so long, and all so troublesome, that it is a saving of time and vexation to get a team.

And now, without fear of further obstruction, we were fairly on our way to Great Barrington. The river seems to pursue a diagonal course over the Great Barrington intervale. We pulled as rapidly as possible, as the shades of evening were beginning to fall, and the cool air was an inducement to keep a-going. The sun after a while disappeared in a cloud of fire behind the Taconic dome which towers two thousand feet above the valley, leaving the slope in view, a solemn mass of darkest green, while Monument Mountain, at the other end of the valley, stood out in a purplish glow, clear and distinct in the still air.

I remember no river scene, indeed, of greater beauty. The stream itself, too, was very beautiful. The banks on either side sloped down to the water's very edge of smooth turf, oft broken, however, by a clump of trees or

Old House at Great Barrington

masses of clustering vines; and we occasionally passed a little inlet, usually guarded by a martial array of cat-o'-nine-tails. Later, the water was smooth as polished black marble, and reflected, with gloomy accuracy, the dark banks and the floating boat whenever we ceased to row. We came to the first bridge, which is just above the dam at Great Barrington, as a tuneful clock in the village was chiming the hour of seven. We tied the boat fast near the west end of the bridge, and having stowed our heavy baggage at a curious, old, rambling, tumble-down house close by, we found shelter at the Berkshire House, a very substantial hotel.

There is a stateliness and dignity about Great Barrington as great in reality as its high-sounding name would imply. It is a rare combination of New-England thrift and New-York opulence. Beecher, it is, I believe, who once declared that he never entered the village without wishing that he was never to leave it. Here Bryant practised law before finally straying into journalism and the more congenial field of literature.

Great Barrington is in the midst of a fine region for drives. The road to the top of Monument Mountain is deservedly in favor, while one of the finest drives in Berkshire is through North Egremont, and then by way of Hillsdale, a town just over the border of Massachusetts, in New York, to Bash-Bish Falls, in Copake. The crest of a hill just above Hillsdale commands a magnificent view of the Catskills and an extensive view of the Berkshire hills, whose broad slopes, blooming with cultivation and beauty, roll upward, in the far distance, beyond a fertile expanse of territory where the valley is widest.

There is another way to Bash-Bish: through South

Egremont, and thence over the mountains; and this is perhaps the most picturesque drive of all. The view of the Taconic range, as one goes westward over the country, which is comparatively level, to the foot of the mountains, is especially fine. The Dome of Mount Everett, alone, remains unchangeable upon its huge, buttress-like foundation, as one draws near; but elsewhere, the mountains break, from time to time, into new and beautifully varying shapes. The view of the Taconics is essentially the same over the Hillsdale road, but the way, as one mounts upward through the valley between the mountains, especially if the day is warm, is, upon the whole, rather more agreeable, and very attractive withal. The music of a brook alongside the road at length dies away, however, and as you emerge from the thick woods, you come upon the now quite famous Goodale Sky Farm, airily perched high up on the mountain-side, where there is a most enchanting view through the verdurous walls of the long valley up which you have just come, and over a beautiful landscape beyond to Greylock, fifty miles distant. Soon thereafter, the head of the valley terminates upon the table-land of the town of Mount Washington, which is surrounded on every side by mountain tops, which peer up here and there, above the edges of the plain, as if they were playing a game of bo-peep.

Soon descending, however, from this high and charming region, the delight of the ubiquitous summer boarder, one hears again, from amidst the shady recesses through which the road, for the most part, wanders, the accompaniment of a running stream, or sees it tumbling over its rocky bed; and opposite Eagle's Nest, just above the head of the Bash-Bish ravine, is a superb view of the towering Catskills, which, as one gazes through the framing walls of the valley, rock-ribbed on one side and densely wooded on the other, look in the distance, beyond the broad and beautiful expanse of country intervening, like blue barriers of eternity.

The name Bash-Bish, which was originally bestowed upon the falls by the Indians, signifies, it is said, Wild Waters. A hotel has been built near the foot of the falls, at the head of the ravine, which is indeed altogether a delightfully wild mountain nook.

CHAPTER III.

GREAT BARRINGTON. — KENT.

EARLY Monday morning we carried the boat around the east end of the dam of the Berkshire Woolen Mills, and put in just below. We threaded our way

among the rocks under the foot-bridge of the mill and a passenger bridge just below, and then swiftly drifted stern foremost through a stretch of rapids, past a deserted mill on one side and the houses of the village opposite. The sun shining on the turbulent water gave it the appearance of molten lead in violent agitation, and it was at times difficult, on account of the perplexing glare, to guide the boat aright among the rocks, though the rapid is not in the least dangerous. We soon came to a bridge

A Crazy Bridge

in the reach below, pulled up under the west end at seven o'clock, and leaving all the baggage in the boat, walked to the hotel, which is at the corner of Bridge Street and Main Street, for breakfast. In the History of Great Barrington, by Charles J. Taylor, it is stated that the bridge is eight hundred and forty-five feet above the level of tide-water.

On our way to the hotel we met a man who would, one would imagine, have little difficulty in proving a mistake of identity if occasion required, as he wore a heavy imperial, one half of which was white and the other red. Six witnesses having looked at him from one side would swear, without a moment's hesitation, and correctly, that he had red whiskers; and another half dozen would swear with equal facility that they were white. The fable of the knight of the gold and silver shield might indeed easily be replaced, in lower Berkshire at any rate, by the instance of the man with the red-and-white imperial.

A little south of the Episcopal Church in the village is an old house, which has been standing unaltered for nearly a century and a half, " the quaintness of its architecture now presenting " — I quote from an unknown correspondent — " a strange and interesting contrast to its modern neighbors. In 1777, General Lincoln and staff were quartered in the house for a few days before being sent with the Massachusetts troops to oppose Burgoyne's advance from Crown Point upon Bennington. Three years later, in 1780, it sheltered Washington on his journey north from Hartford. Within its ancient walls William Cullen Bryant, while practising law in Great Barrington, wooed and wed Miss Fannie Fairchild; a union," the writer adds, " that in every way fulfilled the beauty of its promise." There, also, Bryant wrote Green River, A Walk at Sunset, To the West Wind, and one of his longest and most notable poems, delivered before the Phi Beta Kappa Society of Harvard in 1821, the year of his marriage.

We started again at eight o'clock, and found the going remarkably good, but as remarkably crooked. Language is indeed inadequate to convey an idea of the fantastic turnings of the river. In about an hour we came in sight of the Leavitt Mansion, on the east bank. The river swept by apparently, but soon again turned to the mansion; and then, after rambling about the meadows a while, returned once more, and then gliding under a bridge, which is only two miles from Great Barrington, approached the base of a woody hill, and the mansion finally disappeared as we pulled south through a comparatively long reach. Soon, however, the river turned from the mountain at a point where the steep slope has been denuded of trees, leaving exposed a broad strip of rock-ribbed surface, sharply defined at each edge from base to summit, by dense green woods, — a peculiar transformation that frequently occurs in the valley below Falls Village, — and began to ramble once more in the wide intervale.

By and by we passed the mouth of Green River, a stream celebrated in the verse of Byrant, which was most appropriately named, as its waters are of a decided greenish tinge. The Housatonic itself, transparent as air, reflected every grain of sand and parti-covered gravel and flowing weeds in the channel with luminous softness, except where the current slowly flowed into deep places. Often schools of fish broke from under the boat, scattering in rays like a shower of arrows. Trees lined the banks from time to time, and added constant variety to the continually varying course of the river. It was indeed a place in which to linger; but we pulled on at a steady pace, and after a while passed under a red bridge, just below which is a little fall, and then continued on to an old wooden bridge that leads to the north end of Sheffield Street, a long, shady avenue, with houses on either side.

Sheffield is indeed a handsome old town; but it has a torpid appearance as if it were dozing under its sleepy elms. The municipality of Sheffield, England, would, I have little doubt, pay a round sum, if it could have its namesake transplanted just as it is and set down somewhere in the busy region within its corporate limits. Below, the bed of the stream was occasionally filled with trunks of trees that sometimes almost blocked up our way.

"A half-hour's pull brought us to another long, covered, weather-stained bridge. The road from the west end leads direct to the middle of the village of Sheffield which is only a short distance away. Here we pulled up for a while, and my fellow-voyager, after we had partaken of some sardines, used the oil on his boots and pronounced it good. The river then winds worse than ever, if it were possible, until it approaches a range of hills on the east side of the valley.

whereon are several houses, the first, excepting, perhaps, at rare intervals an isolated building, we had seen since leaving Great Barrington.

We pulled the boat ashore at the end of a reach under the hill and at one of the farm-houses had a sumptuous repast of rye-bread and milk and canned fresh beef we had taken with us. On returning to the boat we found in the brief interval of our absence an entire change had come over the face of nature. The air had been sultry before and we had had a warm time rowing between the high clay-banks which are characteristic of the river below Sheffield. The wind had suddenly veered to the northeast and was cold and raw, mists rolled around the top of the Dome, and clouds were scudding furiously across the sky. We started at two o'clock, and before going a dozen strokes were enveloped in a scanty sprinkle of little rain-drops, and then another until the rain poured in torrents and battered the surface of the river into a long sheet of deep-fretted

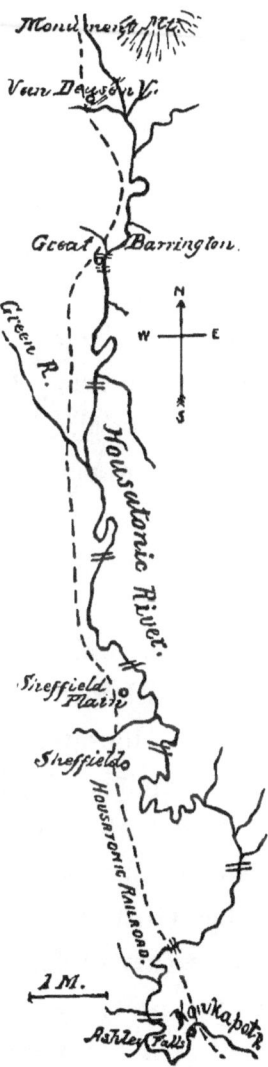

water. We protected ourselves with rubber coats and pulled on, and in about an hour rowed under the road bridge and a railroad bridge which cross the river side by side. The village of Ashley Falls is about a mile distant from the bridges on the east bank. The erratic river then trends across the intervale in long zigzag reaches to a group of houses on the west bank. The wet buildings, exhibiting no signs of life, enveloped in the melancholy haze of rain, looked dreary in the extreme. The reach, immediately below a bridge that spans the river just below the group of houses, ends against the rocky face of a mountain spur that turns the river eastward. The river again approaches the mountain below, however, where a rocky cliff stands guard, and above, a broad field of brown heath, dotted with stones, stretches in grim realistic fashion to the base of woods that crown the summit. The reaches here are all longer and wider, and the banks, which are quite high, were fairly ablaze with brilliant autumnal color. We had often since leaving Housatonic pulled by an uncouth looking scow, lying against the bank, and here we passed a hideous looking craft which had two names. "The Old Sal" was painted on the stern and on the side near the bow, "The Great Eastern, owned and navigated by ———;" an odd vagary of fancy. About five o'clock we saw before us the bridge of the Hartford and Connecticut Western Railroad. Just above it is a short rapid. We landed at a farm-house just below the bridge on the west bank and walked to Canaan, a mile distant on the east side of the river, on the railroad.

Canaan is a sort of Mugby Junction. The tracks of the Hartford and Connecticut Western and Housatonic Railroads intersect at right angles at a corner of the station. There are two hotels in the village, but, apart from the noise of trains, Canaan is not a remarkably lively place.

We got under way Tuesday morning at nine o'clock. The river flows deep and tranquil below the bridge, until it has disappeared around the first bend, where we glided through a gently flowing rapid. We had passed a great many pumpkins afloat on the river from time to time during our morning row and the day preceding, and we had been tempted to use one of the grotesque, dumb yellow masques as a sort of jack-a-lantern ornament to our prow. After a while we pulled under a bridge, and, as we were rowing along close to shore, we discovered at the edge of the water what at first we supposed was the sloughed off skin of a snake, and then the dead root of a tree. It turned out to be, however, the crumpled horns of a skeleton ram's head. We at once made it fast to the bow, and thenceforward had a weird and imposing figure-head.

The river flows in somewhat regular long reaches, with a smooth current, to Falls Village. Twice, however, at a stated interval, the river turns sharply almost northward before resuming its southward sweeps. Mountains guard the valley on either hand, but the intervale and near hills give evidence of careful cultivation. We were indeed passing through the last intervale region on the river. The scenery is not so strikingly beautiful as in the Great Barrington meadows, but the river itself is, if it were possible, more beautiful. At Falls Village, however, the mountains come close to the river, and thereafter remain constant near guardians to the end; and the river is, for the most part, rough and rapid, foaming with only brief intervals of rest through narrow mountain valleys.

We reached Falls Village, which is the gate-way of this wild and lonesome region, at eleven o'clock. The descent of the river from Pittsfield to the State line of Connecticut is two hundred and ninety-five feet, while the descent from the State line to Derby is six hundred and twelve. The actual distance from Pittsfield to the State line is about one third the distance from Pittsfield to the mouth of the river; but the river in Massachusetts, on account of its crooked windings, is about as long as the river in Connecticut.

On account of the low stage of the water, we carried over the rocks of the upper pitch of the falls in the middle of the river, and then, rowing past the repair-shops of the Housatonic Railroad on the west bank, we hauled ashore just above the railroad bridge, and let the boat float along down to the edge of the principal fall.

with a cord. The river makes a plunge here of thirty or forty feet, with considerable roar and blowing spray. We then dragged the boat over the rocks a short distance on the west side, and lowered it over a steep cliff to a ledge below, where, by means of a long cord at the bow, and

At Falls Village.

another at the stern, we let her down to the water at one side of the fall. We tried to run the rapids below the fall, but the channel was narrow and strewn with rocks, and we, therefore, concluded it was the part of discretion to let the boat through with a cord, while we walked along the east side of the principal channel in the middle of the river. Arriving at the end of our footing, we got into the boat and pulled to the west side of the river, where we used the cord once more, to get by the third pitch. Our operations had attracted quite a crowd on the bank, and an entire district school, with the teacher at the head, was narrowly observing every movement. My fellow-voyager then took the oars, as the water was shallow and turbulent, while I walked along the west shore and awaited his coming under the bridge at the village.

Just above the bridge, the channel winds among rocks, and the oarsman, in an endeavor to escape the first one, got the oars out of the row locks, and, before he could replace them to pull back, the boat drifted broadside on a rock that peered out of water immediately below, careened, filled; and the water, rushing into the boat, washed oars, carpet-bags, and all our provisions down stream. The last I saw of my carpet-bag, it was placidly floating in the middle of the river, some distance below, the handle just out of water; and then the waves closed over it. The oarsman stepped on the rock when the boat began to fill, and, after breaking a paddle, all his further efforts to keep her from sliding down still deeper proved unavailing, and the boat finally lodged about a foot under water, and the current, rushing in, held her immovably fast. There was nothing to do but strip and plunge in, and after a half-hour's manoeuvering, the boat was turned over and edged along to another rock, below, where the water poured against the bottom of the boat. The long rope at the stern was then caught and thrown ashore, whereat a man pulled hard, and by half-inches at a time, the boat was hauled into the stream and floated over a short rapid; and after the water was bailed out I put back to the rescue of my fellow-voyager, who stood, to the utter amazement of late comers on the scene, after the boat had got wedged against the second rock under the bridge, dry shod on the upper rock in the middle of the river upon a rather precarious foothold. On getting to shore, he stripped to unmentionables also, and by repeated divings rescued all our canned goods, which glittered in the deep water just below the place of the overturn. Then keeping on down stream with one rescued oar, we fished our carpet-bags out of the stream below, and picked up the other articles a boy had rescued and left on the bank, and started on down river in search of the missing oar. We eventually missed, besides the ram's head, only a few things of no great value. We passed through three reaches of swift water, and then came to a wide, open bay, where, two hours after the accident occurred, we found the oar imbedded in weeds. We had been induced, by the low stage of the water, to try the falls, and naturally were somewhat provoked after getting by the three upper pitches, which are really difficult, — I doubt very much indeed whether they were ever attempted before, — to get wrecked on a couple of paltry rocks at the very end. It is no doubt much better to land above the first pitch on the west side at a solitary barn, and, indeed, quite necessary, I may say, as the water is seldom lower than when we took our trip, and get a team to carry you over the bridge below the lower pitch to the east shore, where it is an easy task to launch a boat in good water.

The scenery below Falls Village, especially just above and below Lime Rock Bridge, is wild and grand. A range of mountains with a very ragged edge stretches away from the river on the west, while mountains covered with green woods slope up from the river on the east. The village of Lime Rock is a mile from the west end of the bridge, and, it is said, contains several fine residences, among others, that of the Hon. W. H. Barnum of State and national reputation.

As we journeyed on we saw many brilliant sunset effects on the mountains along the east side of the narrow valley. Now, upon a dark green slope was outlined, in bright yellow sunshine, the form of one mountain ridge on the west side of the valley, and then again, another. I remember distinctly how the upper part of one long ridge was gilded with brilliant, almost dazzling light, while all the valley below was filled with intense, deep, sombre hues; and we often saw the sun rise and set over the sloping western ridges. The river, most of the time, pours along over fretted stones; and the scenes, as night closed in, were extremely wild, almost weird. The mountain ranges were, for the most part, covered with trees, but occasionally a mountain had been stripped bare, and the naked granite looked desolate and dreary in the extreme. We often saw a strip of bare waste girdling a slope where wood-choppers were still at work, and frequently, near at hand or afar off down the valley, perhaps close to a mountain summit, the flowing smoke of a charcoal pit; and when night added brilliancy to the glow of the fires that flamed here and there on the dark slopes, it seemed as if one were in the midst of one of Grimm's tales, in a land of dragons and gnomes.

About seven o'clock, we saw the twinkling lights of West Cornwall, a decided misnomer, as the village is on the east side of the river, and we made fast just above the dam. We found refuge at the Mansion House, where we were long occupied, both before and after supper, in hanging our wet clothes on a dryer in the kitchen, and were often, I fear, in the way of two young, and pretty, and remarkably lively stepping dames of the domain.

Our shipwreck had opened the seams of the boat considerably, and before embarking next morning, we were engaged, an hour or more, in filling them with cotton batting and putty. While at work, a man told us about a trip that three canoeists from Boston had made down the river the previous year, and pointed out the shed in which they had stored their boats over night. We had heard of the party from the proprietor of the Berkshire

House at Great Barrington; but whether they succeeded in getting through, I know not, although we heard of them once afterward at New Milford. We got under way at ten o'clock. Just above the bridge is a low apron dam. We landed toward the east end, and, in a few minutes, had lowered the boat over the dam and were bumping through

the rapids below. We were obliged to stand up and push with the oars, when opposite the shears factory, and then were hurried, by the swift water, between two mountains that sprang from the water's edge on either side, toward a shallow rapid, which, however, we ran without difficulty. The scenery was quite wild and picturesque, the road along the west shore alone giving a hint that the place was in reach of civilization.

We soon came to other shallow places, however, where we had hard work to get through. One great cause of difficulty was occasioned by fish-ways, which were made up of stones heaped in a long line, usually in a diagonal direction from shore to shore. If we went through the upper end we were quite sure to be stuck on shallows; if, on the other hand, we followed the deeper water along the upper side of the way to the lower end, there was no opening and we had to lift the boat over the stones. Sometimes, however, we found an opening in the wall where we could shove through. The river was often filled with huge rocks, and in a few places the channel was very narrow and the water poured through in a rapid fall. At the worst places we turned the boat around and went through stern foremost. Going through in this way we were enabled, even where the water was very swift and violent, to pull back and keep the boat steady until we had selected the best course. Much of the time one or the other of us walked along the shore. We had indeed altogether rather a tedious forenoon journey, and were three hours in getting to Cornwall Bridge, a distance of five miles. There is quite a high fish-way obstruction just above the bridge at Cornwall Bridge, and we had considerable trouble in getting past. We often wished, indeed, that the river was a foot higher. The water, however, as if to make some compensation, was pure and transparent as crystal.

Below the bridge was another long stretch of shallow water, where my fellow-voyager, alone in the boat, exercised his ingenuity to the utmost to get through. In the next rapid we had no difficulty, as the channel was comparatively narrow, and we rushed through in fine style. We pulled up on the east shore, where the back water curled around to the foot of the rapid and in a sheltered nook enjoyed a lunch after our long fast and hard labor, and were again under way at three o'clock. The going continued to improve, and we soon came to Boardman's Bridge. The road from the east end leads to Cornwall Bridge and the west to Sharon. Below we ran aground two or three times, but the river was less rapid and the country not quite so wild. After a while the river was divided into several channels by graceful islands, and the shadows of evening began to fall upon the

> "Many-color'd woods,
> Shade deep'ning over shade, the country round
> Imbrown; crowded umbrage, dusk, and dun,
> Of every hue, from wan declining green
> To sooty dark."

And then again the fires of charcoal pits illuminated mountain slopes near and remote, and it seemed as if we were sailing through some vast, mysterious region of witchcraft. We still pursued our way in smooth water, however, with some confidence. By and by, we passed the houses of Alder City, on the west bank, whose lights twinkled cheerfully under the black shadow of the Scatacook Mountains, and, upon inquiry by hallooing, learned that we were two miles from Kent, our intended stopping-place. Pursuing our way in the Egyptian darkness, we cautiously approached a huge misshapen object in our course, which proved to be a catamaran. We had before heard a noise like an unearthly groan, repeated at brief regular intervals, and could then hear the water pouring over the dam; so we kept along the east shore, and landed as close to the dam as we dared go. Stumbling along the road, attracted by a feeling of curious horror toward the dreadful moaning, we saw, in front, a furnace, belching flame and sparks from the chimney, and a wing of the building aglow with the lurid, bright glare of a casting. We found that the groaning was due to a water-wheel and wind suction pump that supplied the furnace with air. It was easy, indeed, for a moment, however, upon arrival, to imagine one's self in Hades. We left our baggage in charge of the foreman, and walked half a mile down the track to the Elmore House in Kent.

CHAPTER IV.

KENT. — STRATFORD.

WE had little opportunity to see Kent, but it had all the dignity of an eminently respectable New-England village, in the quiet air of early morning, as we left it still asleep on our way to the boat. We carried the boat around the dam on a wheelbarrow, and, relying upon the statement of a workman, put the boat in the tail-race, and, having loaded the baggage, embarked ourselves. The race was narrow and the current swift, and the boat got athwart the stream under a low-lying, projecting tree and filled, and all the baggage was washed out and got wet. Furthermore, after getting righted, we found that the race at the end expanded into shallows, — which, however, had never been the case before, — that would have made a carry necessary in any event; so we were not at all obliged to our informant. We easily rescued everything, however, including a can of julienne soup. We were continually reserving the julienne for a choice occasion, but after losing it in both our overturns, we carried it the length of the river, and, sad to relate, brought it home unused. However, we finally got under way about ten o'clock, and soon pulled under the bridge at Kent, which will, I doubt not, be a better structure hereafter, as it was undergoing repairs.

The river banks are somewhat more open below Kent. On the east side, indeed, was quite a stretch of intervale. The reaches were long and graceful, and it was very delightful rowing in the clear air of an autumn morning. The trees were flaming in gorgeous colors, the maples, most brilliant of all, fairly ablaze with crimson and gold. The shrubbery was usually very gay, and, most beautiful of all, the vines of various colors creeping around the trunks of trees. The soft haze of an Indian summer was on the hills, and the air was deliciously cool. We arrived above the upper pitch of Bull's Falls at twelve o'clock, and landed on the east shore where we luckily, at once, found a team to transport us around. Bull's Falls is not a very large place. There is a store, one white house, and two or three red ones. A survey of the Housatonic was made last year for the purpose of determining the availability of the river as a source from which to increase the water supply of the city of New York, and the report was, I believe, favorable, and contemplated the location of a great reservoir at Bull's Falls.

A friend of the writer, who, in company with another, had navigated the river in a small skiff, in the third week of July, 1879, and unfortunately suffered shipwreck at Lover's Leap below, said he ran the first pitch of Bull's Falls, though it was the worst place he passed through on the river, and added, in a list of directions which we found very useful, in a somewhat humorous tone: "The lower pitch is truly terrific, and is best seen from the bridge. The river pours down a ledge to a depth so great that everything below seems dwarfed in the awful abyss." The river pours through a very narrow channel of rocks at an angle of about forty-five degrees, and finds rest before again plunging onward in a pond behind a deserted dam just below the bridge. We rode a mile and a half, and then, at a place where the road approached the river, launched the boat within sight of Gaylord's Bridge. We paid for the transportation of ourselves and boat, seventy-five cents. We backed the boat through a bad stretch of rapids under the bridge, and thence made good progress on our way to New Milford. A white church with a square tower, on a little elevation on the west side of the bridge, continued in view quite a long time, a prominent picturesque object, like a church in a picture. While rowing along, we came upon a flock of ducks in a cove, which, perhaps luckily for them and perhaps fortunately for us, proved to be tame, as they came within range.

Hitherto, our course from Falls Village had been in a wild, rough, mountainous region. I doubt, indeed, whether we passed through a mile of country, in all, that could be considered intervale, and a cultivated field was about as rare as intervale. We had mountains, rocks, trees, and a river that every few hundred feet was a foaming rapid. There is, indeed, an almost endless series of unused water privileges on the Housatonic, easily capable, it would seem, of being improved. It was, therefore, a relief to find the encircling mountains give way, and a broad open tract of country gradually disclosing itself before us as we drew near New Milford. Rounding a bend, we saw the houses of the village scattered over the side of a hill, looking, at a distance, much like a toy village. We were quite puzzled, for a time, to discover the use of several barrels painted white and apparently located as beacons along the river; but, as we pulled ashore below the bridge, we found a small paddle-wheel steamer, not much larger than a row-boat, at anchor, and we inferred that they were planted to aid it in navigating the broad and placid shallows opposite the town.

New Milford is the centre of trade for a large district, and it is very active and thriving. All the villages above are small — mere settlements; and the nearest villages below, on the river, are Derby and Birmingham, which are twenty-eight miles distant. The predominance of English names in the valley of the Housatonic is very noticeable. We stopped at the New England House, a hotel where the white-haired landlord is exceedingly jolly, lunch is always on the table, and the fare is excellent.

We pushed off at seven o'clock next morning. The river was enveloped in a thick mist. We kept close to the east shore, and soon heard the water pouring over a low dam which is, perhaps, half a mile below the bridge. We passed the mouth of the canal that leads to the mill, which we had been warned to avoid, and landed at the east end of the dam and carried the boat over a convenient rocky ledge, and then, holding her by the cord, let her float through the short rapids below. While thus engaged, we found a half dozen large eels that had been caught in a trap at the end of a fish-way. There are so many fish-ways on the river, however, that I should think the catch everywhere must ordinarily be small.

Pulling under the railroad bridge below, where the Housatonic Railroad crosses the river for the last time, we continued on in the middle of the stream. The reaches were wide and long, and the trees on either side loomed vaguely through the dissolving mist, like gigantic ghosts. We had been approaching a mountain range directly in our path, and after about an hour's pull, we saw before us the dreaded Lover's Leap where the river makes its way through a wild gorge. On the right bank, just above, is the mouth of the Danbury River, crossed by a brown bridge. There is a fall of twelve or fifteen feet in the Housatonic just above the gorge, and a bridge crosses the river, just below the fall, at the entrance of the chasm. Between the fall in the middle of the river and the east end of the bridge is a ledge of rocks, and between this ledge and the shore is the narrow channel of a fish-way. We had come to consider Lover's Leap as the critical point of our voyage, for the friend who had supplied us with directions had been compelled to abandon his trip at this point, and he said: "I cannot exaggerate the difficulties of Lover's Leap. The boat cannot be taken out of the stream, for the banks are enormously high and steep where they are not mere cliffs. Furthermore, there is

no road over the mountain, and you will see that it is too high to take a boat over. The fish-way runs between two flat ledges, from one of which rises the cliff; the other is out in the stream, and cannot be reached. The only way to reach the one next to shore is to climb the bank where the bare rock begins. I tried to go along the base of the cliff, and narrowly escaped drowning. I then climbed down the bare cliff to the ledge, no easy or safe job." The river must have been very high at the time he attempted to get through. He said, indeed, that "the water foamed in the fish-way as if it would pull the ring and staple out of the boat." The friend who was with him undertook to lower the boat with the painter through the fish-way from above, so that he could reach her, standing on the ledge below. The rope unluckily proved too short, and the boat rushed by and was swamped on a huge boulder at the end of the way. He added: "Down the gorge all is plain; but at the lower end are ominous breakers, of which I know nothing, and they might drown you, after all, for all I can tell." We landed on the outer ledge and found the fish-way merely a trickling rill. We made a fire in a very convenient cavity on the outer ledge and had the standard repast of the camper-out, beefsteak, roasted potatoes, and coffee. While breakfasting, we glanced, from time to time, down through the gorge where we could see the "ominous breakers" at the end, and get a glimpse of the country beyond, too, like a haven of rest, open, peaceful, and smiling.

We lowered the boat over the rocks beside the fall without any trouble, and, embarking just below, passed under the bridge which crosses the river high in air, and entered the Ausable-like chasm. It is, indeed, a wild and lonesome place, full of rugged beauty. The river is, however, comparatively smooth, except that there are two rapids at the very end of the gorge. We might easily have run the first, but instead, lowered the boat through on the west side with the cord. The other rapid we avoided by guiding the boat through shallow channels on the east side. As you emerge from the chasm, cliffs tower abruptly from the water at each side. The rugged cliff on the west side is covered with a scanty growth of trees, while the other is a bare, rocky steep, crowned with a dead pine, which enhances its desolate appearance. The river below spreads out in quite a wide basin called the Cove. The view of the Leap given is from the lower end, looking north.

We had supposed that, below the gorge, we should have smooth, deep water and level country. We found, however, instead, that the river was rapid and stormy, and ran through a valley, between mountains, amid scenery quite as wild and grand as above New Milford. We occasionally came across a troublesome shallow place, and often the inevitable fish-way, where we invariably had an interchange of opinion as to the best course to take. The going was very good, however, for the most part. After rowing nearly three hours, we saw a board nailed to a tree at the edge of a thick woods on the west bank, and, drawing near, found that it was a memorial, marking the place where a young man had been found dead. Not far below, we pulled up on the west shore where a brook trickled into the river at the edge of a gravelly point, and had our mid-day lunch. Immediately below the point is a shallow fall, and then a bridge. Rowing on, we came, in a little less than an hour, to the bridge of the Shepaug Railroad, which crosses the stream at a lonely place. We passed through a long stretch of rapids above and below the bridge, and then pulling around a very pretty bend bordered along the west side with trees, we came to a low dam which we passed at the west end. Then followed swift currents and rapids. The river, by and by, made a sharp turn eastward, running on the lower side along a finely curving wooded slope. The river continued to follow the spur of the mountain until it seemed to flow almost north, and then debouched into a small, open valley, a place quite as beautiful as any we saw on the trip. The river, as if relieved after its continual fretting over rocks, murmurs pure and limpid over a gravelly bed in a charming little intervale, while two large, white, comfortable looking houses on the north shore attest an appreciation of the charms of the little valley. At the end of the reach below, just above an island, is a ford where we saw a horse drawing a wagon and splashing, with slow contentment, through the shallow water. At the extreme end of the same reach is the truss bridge of the New York and New England Railroad, which, perched on lofty stone piers, spans the river like an aerial spider's web. The river below flows rapidly around a perfectly curving wooded bank. A few minutes after six o'clock, we came to Bennett's Bridge, where an island divides the river and bridge. We pulled under the eastern section and, landing on the gravel shore below, found shelter at the boarding-house of H. M. Post.

We started next morning at seven o'clock, and found the river about as usual, only the reaches were longer and broader, and the distance from rapid to rapid a little farther, while mountains still bordered the narrow valley on every side. We also got stuck two or three times in shallow places. We reached Zoar's Bridge, where a very handsome chain suspension bridge spans the river, about ten o'clock. Then, after passing through several rapids where the full current ran delightfully swift in narrow channels, we came to the head of a long pond formed by the Derby-Birmingham dam which sets the water back between six and seven miles. Here we encountered a violent southwest wind, and were glad to keep under the lee of mountains wherever they afforded protection. The scenery about the pond is essentially the same as along the river, embracing principally mountains, woods, and water. There is, however, some cultivated land, and a few houses are scattered along the shores. The pond is comparatively narrow, gradually widening, however, as you approach the end; and, as we rounded the last bend, a magnificent broad expanse of water stretched before us to the dam. Beyond the gate-house on the west side rises the tall brick tower of the Derby mills, and a few scattering houses are visible on the high ground on both sides below. There is a lock at the gate-house, but the keeper was not at hand and we had no time to hunt him up, so we pulled to the east end of the dam and there made a portage. A wide, deep, unused canal leads off from the east end of the dam, over which we carried the boat on a narrow stone walk on the east side of the gate-house.

The dam is a very imposing structure of stone, twenty-two feet high, with the lower face nearly perpendicular. It is six hundred and thirty-seven feet long, in the form of a curve, which is fifty feet deep, with the concave side facing down stream. In a history of Derby I find a statement that the trembling sound of the water pouring over the dam, when the river is full, has been observed in the upper part of the city of New Haven, a distance, in a direct line, of over eight miles. There is a lock on the west bank, just above the Derby mills, between the canal and river. The bank below is lined with mills to the bridge, while on the east side below the bridge are the factories and houses of Birmingham, which is located on a tongue of land between the Housatonic and Naugatuck Rivers. The river forms quite a basin immediately below the bridge, and several schooners, at wharves, and a sharpy, darting here and there, warned us of our approach to the sea.

We began our last pull on the river about two o'clock. We kept close to the west shore, under the shelter of mountainous wooded slopes, whenever it was possible, to avoid, as far as we could, the wind, which was fiercely blowing. The tide, luckily, was with us. Still our progress was slow. The river is several hundred feet wide, and the reaches very picturesque. The shore was rocky and wooded almost all the way to Stratford. We occasionally pulled by a little beach ensconced between rocks, and sometimes an open space wherein a house was prettily located. A fence projecting into the stream often compelled us to make a brief detour, and by and by we passed little fleets of moored dories, and huge reels in sheltered coves, and many a fine camping place, of which, however, there had been no lack all along the river. There were marshes here and there, and yet, although we were so near the sea, and the tide was running strong, the water was fresh. Late in the afternoon we saw a long way off down river, over a wide expanse of water beyond a marsh, the high crossed framework of a long bridge outlined against the sky, and the spires of Stratford. The banks were dark and sombre, the water in the channel a raging mass of white caps, while heavy clouds rent and torn by the furious wind were scudding along above, lighted with the gorgeous and continually changing hues of a brilliant sunset, the entire scene resembling very much a sullen and angry Turner.

We pulled under the truss bridge of the New York and New Haven Railroad about six o'clock. We continued on, however, to the Washington toll-bridge just below, on the old post route from Boston to New York, which, it is said, derives its name from the fact that Washington marched over it when on his way to New York after the British evacuated Boston. There is a hotel at the east end of the bridge. The river below the toll-bridge flows past the Lower Dock at Stratford, as it is called, and then a mile further in a magnificent wide, semi-circular sweep between level marshes to the sea. The mouth of the river is guarded on the eastern side by Milford Point, where there is a hotel, and on the west by a light-house. The town of Milford is on the east bank, but the village is three miles from the bridge. Stratford is on the west side, about a mile from the river. It is a large old-fashioned village with wide, rambling, well-shaded streets. Many of the houses are covered with long, wide shingles, and the windows are filled with the small panes of glass anciently in vogue. There is no factory in the village and no hotel. It is, therefore, as one would naturally suppose, a very quiet place, and it has a quaint and extremely conservative air, which the modern houses cannot dispel. Bridgeport is three miles west of Stratford, and New Haven thirteen miles east.

We were seven days in all in descending the river, which may be considered the utmost limit of time necessary, as the water was almost unprecedentedly low and the days short. The invigorating autumn air, however, enabled us to sustain the burden of rowing, which some one has characterized as the easiest kind of hard work, — as it surely is for one accustomed to it, though a most grievous task to a novice, — with an effective stroke from morning until night. The friend who supplied us with directions, upon hearing an account of our trip wrote: " I did not suppose we had such very high water, and it could not have been very high in July either. I am sure that letting down over the great falls at Falls Village would have been about as practicable for us as letting down by Niagara. We were less than three quarters of an hour in going from West Cornwall to Cornwall Bridge, where you seem to have had so much trouble. We rushed right along, bow on, as I never rushed on any stream before. At Lover's Leap the fishway was a roaring torrent, and the waves at the end were tremendous curlers. With the same stage of water I do not believe that it would be safe to undertake to go through."

I should advise any one in boating on the Housatonic not to be in a hurry, if possible to avoid it. It is a beautiful stream from beginning to end. Whoever descends it, indeed, in whatever way, will undoubtedly retain in memory unfading visions of scenes of rare beauty, which he will nevertheless unhappily find as impossible to describe as the charms of a perfect poem or a perfect picture.

A single word of caution: Be sure you know how to handle oars in wild water before embarking on the mad Housatonic.

THE NASHUA RIVER.

CHAPTER I.

WEST BOYLSTON. — LANCASTER.

"Where through the calm repose
Of cultured vales and fringing woods the gentle Nashua flows."
                                                WHITTIER.

AT the end of the trip on the Housatonic I had the boat sent as freight to West Boylston on the South Branch of the Nashua, in Worcester County, and in July of the following year took the three o'clock train from Boston on the Boston and Albany Railroad, with a friend of previous experience in river travel, to make a voyage in her down the Nashua. At Worcester, after a very convenient interval of forty minutes between trains, which we improved by making additions to our store of supplies, we took the five o'clock train on the Worcester and Nashua Railroad.

After a short ride of twenty-four minutes we landed at West Boylston, and, without delay, obtained of the station-agent the bill of freight for the boat, which amounted to six dollars and fifty-five cents. The charge of the New York, New Haven, and Hartford Railroad from Stratford to Springfield, a distance of seventy-five miles, was one dollar and seventy-five cents; that of the Boston and Albany for transporting her from Springfield to

Worcester, fifty-six miles, three dollars and twenty cents, while the charge of the Worcester and Nashua for nine miles was one dollar and sixty cents.

The boat weighed only about one hundred and fifty pounds, but was rated by the first road as weighing seven hundred. The Boston and Albany, however, was much more generous and had rated her as weighing two thousand pounds. The rate for a boat on the printed tariff of the Worcester and Nashua Railroad is fifteen hundred pounds, but the Worcester and Nashua in a magnanimous spirit lost sight of its own rating and adopted, by some strange preference, that of the Boston and Albany instead of the somewhat more reasonable fiction of the New York, New Haven, and Hartford.

Having briefly called the attention of the agent to the somewhat remarkable variability of rates for such an apparently extraordinary article of carriage as our boat, we discovered, upon lowering her from a long enforced retirement on rafters in the loft of the freight-house, and bringing her to the light of day, that she had been badly damaged in transportation. There was a yawning crevice nearly seven feet long on one side close to the bottom. The seams were of course all open, but we had foreseen that they probably would be, and had provided ourselves with means to make them tight. It was necessary, however, to procure a skilful workman to repair the injury, and, upon inquiry, we were directed to the wheelwright,

Mr. Goselin. We carried the boat with our baggage on a wheelbarrow, with alternate reliefs in wheeling, down a pretty steep road from the dépôt, and across the level of a narrow valley to Goselin's shop, which is on the bank

West Boylston.

of the river. Goselin examined the break carefully, and then with a calm, judicial air that was eminently reassuring said he could repair it on the morrow.

Just beyond Goselin's a handsome stone bridge with stone parapets spans the Nashua, and only a few steps away is an ordinary wooden one over a canal. Immediately beyond the canal is a small, unpretentious hotel, which, however, unluckily, happened to be closed; and, as it is the only one in town, we were compelled to seek quarters for the night at a remote private house, — while farther on, past a row of buildings, in front of which is a park, that might, perhaps, be considered extensive in Lilliput, at the end of the road, is an old, two-storied, double-gabled, red brick building, under a steep hillside, in the longest block of buildings in town.

The view southward from the lower village is exceedingly beautiful. The intervale stretches away in broad and fertile meadows of rich, dark green, bordered on the west by a wooded bank, broken, at a distance, by a projecting headland of bare earth, to a line of high curving hills a couple of miles distant, where a white church-spire gives relief to thickly-wooded slopes. The river flows in graceful curves over the broad expanse, its course marked here and there by a bordering of trees, while at the extreme end of the vale, where the hills crowd together, hangs a high red bridge. The canal runs along the easterly side of the intervale, and half a mile away, at the end of a wooded bank, close under a hill, stands, entirely by itself, in a grand sort of way, the large brick building of the Clarendon Mills. There is a bridge at the upper village, which is perhaps a third of a mile above the stone bridge, and just below it is the dam of Holbrook's Mill.

THE NASHUA RIVER.   133

It would be easy to carry a boat by the dam, and in taking a trip on the river it would be well to begin at least as high up as Oakdale, the next station above West Boylston, on the Worcester and Nashua Railroad, where the Quinepoxet River from Holden and the Stillwater from Sterling, unite to form the South Branch of the Nashua; and, generally, the higher up a river one can

Holbrooks Mill.

begin in boating, provided only it is navigable, the better.

Furthermore, since taking this trip the Massachusetts Central Railroad has been completed to Oakdale, and furnishes the most direct route thither from Boston. The station at West Boylston is alongside the canal.

The high ground between the upper and lower villages at West Boylston commands, at most points, a fine view of the broad intervale below; the river, lying deep and quiet like a narrow pond between picturesque banks, while the shapely peak of Wachusett stands forth prominently in the north, only a few miles distant, and adds a mountainous flavor to the gentle beauty of all the rural landscape round. The view from the summit of Mount Wachusett, which is easily accessible, is one of the finest, in extent and variety, of any in Massachusetts.

Early in the afternoon of next day, the boat was ready, so, after preparing and eating lunch in the blacksmith shop which adjoins Monsieur Goselin's establishment, we put her in the canal, as the river itself, on account of the large volume of water drawn off through the canal, was, as we had ascertained, too shallow in many places for navigation. In spite of repairs and caulking, the boat leaked pretty badly at first; but we loaded the baggage and cast off about three o'clock. The canal is wide enough to row in, and there is a good current. We soon came, however, to a bridge so close to the water that we could not pass under it, and we therefore made a portage over it.

The canal then opened into a small pond, bordered on the left with a shady road lined with oblong, box-like boarding-houses. As we pulled down the pond we had a fine view, from its high level, of the intervale opposite and below.

We landed on the embankment at the foot of the pond, and carried the boat over a grassy slope between the

buildings of the Clarendon Mills and the canal, and put
her into the race-way just below, and in a few minutes
were going at a lively rate in a very swift current
between banks of uniform hight, marked alternately with
greenery and patches of gravel.

Canal at West Boylston.

After a while, however, we came to a barrier in the
shape of a log, which for a few minutes looked troublesome. My friend, however, got out and, without much
difficulty, lifted one end of the log, and the boat glided
under without any disturbance to the baggage, which was

heaped up in quite a mountainous pile in the bow. Shortly below, swiftly going with the rushing current, we came to another bridge so low that we could not pass it, and we were again compelled to make a carry, which, however, we quickly accomplished.

The canal thereafter assumed much more the appearance of a river as it flowed, with frequent turns, rapidly between low, open banks, often bordered on both sides with a thick network of bushes. After a delightful sail of about two miles in all, in the canal, the boat drifting stern foremost all the while and the oars only used to keep the course, we emerged into the river, narrow, deep, swift-flowing, and bordered with trees.

We sought here to get a glimpse of the Red Bridge which hangs so high in graceful suspense, in the view from the head of the intervale at West Boylston, but could discover no trace of it, and its later whereabouts remained a mystery of the voyage. We soon passed a high sand-bank on the left, and then, after a few windings, glided through refreshing, cool shadows, under Carr's Bridge, an ancient, weather-stained structure of quaint gracefulness, made still more attractive by the beauty of its shaded approaches. The road south leads to Boylston Centre.

Below, the river was bordered on the right by a steep, woody bank, while opposite were open fields. By and by we passed gravel embankments of the Massachusetts Central Railroad on the right, and after a while pulled between piles upon which the railroad is carried over the river, and entered the pond above Sawyer's Mill.

We pulled under a bridge near the end of the pond, and landed at the left of the dam just below. We found, however, that, upon this occasion at any rate, it would be

Old Bridge at Boylston

easier to get over the dam on the right-hand side, as water was not pouring over the dam and there is quite a high ledge of rocks below the dam on that side. It took us only a few minutes indeed to lower the boat into the river below the dam, and, having reloaded the baggage, we made rapid progress down stream. The Nashua indeed flows very swiftly here, wandering in a charming, vagrant fashion hither and thither over the level of quite an extensive valley, dashing at frequent intervals over beds of gravel and making music as it goes. It was past six o'clock, and we talked of halting to pitch the tent, but, tempted by the pleasant windings of the swift-flowing stream, we continued on and neglectfully passed one good camping ground after another.

While shooting through a rapid at a lively pace we came near being impaled on a barbed wire stretched across the stream. There was quite a number of such wires at various points along the river, and they constitute the only source of danger I know of on the "gentle" Nashua.

After a while the shallow rapids came to a sudden end, and we entered the head of the long pond above Clinton. We soon pulled under a bridge and past a primitive steamboat landing below, and then began to look out in earnest for the night's resting-place, but for a long time without discovering a location in any way desirable. We finally got into the broad pond and at last halted on the left shore, and pitched our tent in the woods on the level of the bank above, and while regretting opportunities for camping neglected above the head of the pond, congratulated ourselves as darkness set in that we had found a place not quite so bad as we had just before come to believe would have to be our refuge. Before going to sleep we could plainly hear conversation and the noise of wagons on the high-road on the opposite side of the pond, and during the night were startled at times into half-conscious wakefulness by the intermittent tread of some creature near the tent.

We got under way about nine o'clock Wednesday. After a short pull between the high banks near the foot of the pond, which diminishes in width toward the end, we landed on the sloping edge of the dam, as water was not pouring over it. The dam, which is just below a bridge, is of stone, not wide, but upwards of twenty feet high. There is no opportunity to get by the dam on either side; it was also quite impossible to lower the boat down its perpendicular face, and we had no inducement to attempt it, as the bed of the stream below was completely dry: so we pulled back past a propeller and two or three sail-boats moored in a group and landed on the north shore near a wharf, and then had to walk up the long hill to the village before we could find a team to carry us around. We drove past the Lancaster Mills,—and out of the long array of buildings came an infernal clatter,—and then along a very fine level road, which at one point runs close to the river. We might have launched the boat here on the brimming flood, but the teamster advised us that there was another dam only a quarter of a mile below, so we continued on, and in a few minutes drove across the road below it, and then shot the boat down a sloping bank, lined with great trees, into the river.

After embarking, it seemed to us, as we looked up stream under the bridge, as if it would not be at all difficult to get by the second dam, which is so low, indeed, that I believe we might have floated the boat over it. We had made considerable saving in time, however, by the long carry, which cost for ourselves, boat, and baggage, about a half mile in all, seventy-five cents. A rapid current bore us swiftly on in an open intervale with high hills at a little distance on almost every side. The houses of Clinton were scattered over the more remote western slopes, with here and there a window glittering in the rays of the sun, and all tremulous in the heat, looking so hot and uncomfortable that we were glad to turn to the swift movement of the coolly flowing river. The current after a little while, however, subsided in the still water of a pond. We supposed at the time that the North Branch of the Nashua here joined the one on which we were sailing, and we looked doubtfully from time to time into the numerous green recesses in which the pond abounded. Fortunately, however, we kept rightly on our way to the foot of it where there is a bridge, with a grist-mill, a homely, old-fashioned building which outwardly gives indication of its use, on one side, while on the right, opposite, is a hill of graceful slope, marked by a great elm and crowned by a farm-house. There is no village in sight, but the place, I believe, goes by the name of South Lancaster. We made a portage, which was very easy, to the right of the bridge, to avoid the dam, which is beneath it. The dam is not very high, but the edge is lined at brief intervals with stakes, which divide the fall of water in a very pretty way into innumerable glass-like portions.

Mill at South Lancaster

We lowered the boat over a little ledge of rocks below the fall, and, while backing her down stream, had our attention attracted to a man on the bridge, who was wildly gesticulating, as his voice was useless in explanation, on account of the noise of the water. We quickly concluded, however, as we were hurrying along in the swift water, and keeping a sharp lookout for our course, that he was trying to tell us about danger on the river, of which we had no fear, and we, therefore, gave him but momentary heed. In a few minutes, we pulled through an arch, under a lofty embankment of the Lancaster Railroad. The road was designed to give Lancaster direct communication with Boston; and was completed to Hudson, but never used. It is now, however, I understand, operated as a branch of the Old Colony, which is thus considerably estray, as it were, from Cape Cod and Plymouth County.

The Nashua then flowed mostly with a swift current, with many a crook and turn over the wide level of a fertile valley. The river now glided gently between turfy banks, and, again, rippled along with soft murmurs; or, descending a bed of gravel, "made music on its pebbled rim." Here and there was a tree or a clump of bushes, while the hills which bordered the valley were silent in a motionless, sleepy haze.

Just above Atherton Bridge, the novel spectacle of a boat on the river, attracted and held the undivided attention of a man and two boys who were sifting gravel on the bank. They gazed with such friendly, sympathetic interest, until we were lost to sight, that I wish we might have taken them in. Below the bridge, we came upon an artist on the left bank, under a white cotton umbrella, painting, perhaps a group of cattle at the water's brink, or some noble trees, or the rich expanse of the broad and luxuriant Lancaster intervale beyond.

The river quickly sent us on our way as it rushed from bank to bank, and in a few minutes we were hurried down a swift rapid to the mouth of the North Branch of the Nashua, a tranquil, dignified stream that seemed like a reproof to check the other's boisterous flow. Pulling out from the current, we landed at the edge of the ripple on a sand beach, at the point of junction, a very delightful spot. Just in front, looking down stream, is the Centre Bridge, which spans the united rivers, while in the rear, between the two branches, stretches a lordly field of more than two hundred acres, bordered on the north by a wooded slope, and marked in the middle by a gigantic oak. The banks of the rivers are lined with trees, which congregate in a little assembly at the point. We pitched the tent here, near the smoothly flowing, dark-brown water of the North Branch. A little distance above was the bridge of the Worcester and Nashua Railroad; and beyond the easterly end, we caught a glimpse here and there, amid banks of foliage, of the houses of Lancaster.

It was past noon, and we began to make preparations for lunch, when we discovered that our can of milk was missing, and then, alas! somewhat too late, we knew the meaning of the rude pantomime by the man on the bridge at South Lancaster. He had endeavored to warn us that we had left it on the bank. It was idle to think of rowing back up the swift stream, so we returned by way of the railroad, under the hottest of July suns, and, luckily, found the can in the cleft of a rock, a little to one side the place of our embarkation, still in plain sight from both road and river. The Nashua is, however, I believe, the Lethe of New England rivers. We were often, indeed, lulled into a state of forgetfulness, in following its mazy windings. At the outset, we forgot a pipe, then the ridge-pole and supports of the tent, and at Lancaster left the hatchet.

Late in the afternoon, we pulled up the North Branch. We rowed under the railroad bridge and the Sprague Bridge just above, and then toiled through a stretch of rapids. We pulled up half a mile perhaps in all, and then turning about, glided swiftly through one rapid after another, with only an occasional stroke, hardly necessary, save to give direction, where thirty or forty hard strokes had barely sufficed to carry us laboriously up. We landed at the Sprague Bridge, and, after rambling through the village, returned to our camp at the junction.

The North Branch of the Nashua is, as maps indicate, a very tortuous stream. I have little doubt, however, that, with a light boat, and no disinclination to an occasional "easy," by wading where the rapids are shallow as well as swift, one could go up as far as Leominster, which is eight miles above Lancaster, and, perhaps, to Fitchburg. It is, however, I have no doubt, easily navigable in descent, from either place, by skiff or canoe.

We rowed up the North Branch again, in the evening, and landed at the foot of a lane, immediately below the railroad bridge. Returning late from the village, we had to grope our way cautiously through the lane, which was very dark; and the river was so black that we could not see a boat's length in any direction. The voyage to camp was, indeed, throughout, a nocturne of shadows.

CHAPTER II.

LANCASTER. — GROTON.

WE were awakened Thursday morning by the sound of great rain-drops heavily pattering on our canvas covering, and were compelled to lie a long time on our beds of hay, in which was mingled much odorous sweet-fern, listening to the music of the storm. The lightning was incessant and vivid, and crash after crash of thunder broke through the sky. It seemed, indeed, as if the ghostlike mythicals whom local tradition says make thunder among the Catskills by bowling ten-pins during a shower, had transferred the scene of their sport, and were bowling a constant succession of strikes above Lancaster. We did not get wet in the least, however, and after a while the thunder rolled grumbling away in the distance, the sun shone brightly, and birds everywhere filled the air with the melody of their delayed matins.

Camp duties were performed by the middle of the morning, and then once more, and for the last time, we pulled up the North Branch to the village. At the landing at the foot of the lane we had talk with a man who, in a communicative humor, told us something of his life. He had been a sailor in his youth, and had voyaged over nearly all the oceans of the world; but now, in middle age, had found a snug harbor in the rural quietude of Lancaster. We had already before, strangely enough, yet naturally, too, perhaps, in accordance with a law that seems to group incidents of a similar kind in life in close sequence, met, in the course of our brief excursion, a reminiscence of the sea, a sailor lad on the train from Boston, who wore the cap of the Powhattan. He was a mere boy, but said he had been away cruising the past nine years. He had written to his parents only once during all this time, and had not heard from them at all. With sailor-like unconcern, however, he was then on his way to Springfield, on a three days' leave of absence, to ascertain whether his home was still unbroken. I should not be at all surprised if he, too, sometime in the future, found a retreat somewhere along the "gentle" Nashua.

The principal part of Lancaster lies upon the westerly slope of a ridge that extends in a northerly direction from the North Branch of the Nashua, and affords a fine view of the river-basin and especially the broad, gently sloping hillsides beyond. Upon the back of the ridge, along its highest elevation, which also commands a wide view of the valley east, are the schoolhouse, Town Hall, Memorial Hall, a church, and a large hotel, all of substantial brick. The town library, a large and well-appointed institution, second only in size and equipment, I think, to the Concord library, is in a very handsome octagonal room in Memorial Hall. Most other towns have, during the past thirty years, felt the impulse of the march of modern times, and now throb with new industries and teem with alien population; but Lancaster preserves, in a marked degree, the traditional character of the old New-England village, and seems likely to for many a year to come. A singularly beautiful rural landscape, which, soon after the landing of the Pilgrims brought the first settlers to the town, still remains its greatest attraction.

Lancaster is indeed the oldest town in Worcester County. It was settled in 1645, and incorporated in 1653. It was for many years the most advanced post of the Pilgrim Colony. The inhabitants, however, lived on amicable terms with the Indians, and the settlement thrived continuously until the outbreak of King Philip's War. On August 22, 1675, eight persons were killed by the Indians, and the tenth of February following, several tribes, led by Philip himself, made a desperate attack upon the town, in five different places at once, in which more than fifty were killed or taken prisoners. Six weeks afterward all the houses but two were destroyed, the town was deserted, and Lancaster remained without an inhabitant for more than three years. The inhabitants then began to return, and were not molested in the resettlement of the town until after King William's accession to the throne of England, which occasioned a new series of hostilities, in which the Indians were encouraged and aided by the French as allies. They made an assault in

July, 1692, and renewed their attacks at various intervals from time to time, down to August 5, 1710, when, as an ancient chronicler says, the *last mischief* was done.

At the time of the assault, in February, 1676, the wife of the minister was taken captive by the Indians, and remained among them several weeks before she was ransomed. Soon after her release she wrote an account of the attack upon the town and her experience among the Indians, which was published in a little book entitled Narrative of the Captivity and Removes of Mary Rowlandson. It is written in quaint language in graphic style and contains a strange admixture of events most pathetic, and incidents most ludicrous, despite their tragic, rueful aspect. The sentences for the most part, however, fairly roll and groan under the burden of her terrible story. The narrative, brief as it is, nevertheless throws a great deal of light on the character, traits, mode of life, and manners of the Indians, and may indeed wisely be read as a very effective antidote to the romanticism of Cooper.

A History of Lancaster was written by the Rev. A. P. Marvin, and published by the town in 1879. It is a very interesting account of the early settlement and progress of the town, and contains many illustrations and maps.

After a while we returned to the junction again, broke camp, and were soon under way once more. We pulled into the ripple swiftly flowing out of the South Branch, and quickly shot under the Centre Bridge, which spans the

Nashua. The Centre Bridge, one hundred and seventy-three feet long, is an iron structure, in suspense from bank to bank, light, graceful, and commodious. The Sprague Bridge over the North Branch, which, in old deeds, was called the North River, is one hundred and forty feet in length; while the Atherton Bridge over the South Branch is ninety.

The main river was called Pennacook by the Indians. The Indian name was retained for a while by the early settlers, according to Marvin's History, and the river is indeed thus designated on the oldest maps. The present name, Nashua, is a corruption of Nashaway, which was the name of the tribe of Indians who lived along the banks of the river, and was after a time, perhaps naturally, and at any rate very happily, bestowed upon it by the settlers. I have seen it stated that *nashaway* was a generic Indian word and signified "a place between" or "in the middle." I have, however, also seen it stated that the word signified "the beautiful stream with the pebbly bottom." The river near Lancaster was also at one time called the Lancaster River, and in the same way the river for an indefinite distance above and below Groton was called the Groton River.

The river at first flowed, for the most part, steadily with a deep strong current between gently curving banks of uniform hight, and we rowed along at an easy pace under a cloudy sky. Standing up in the boat we could look across the broad, luxuriant, level fields to the hills far away on the south side beyond. We often passed a group of cows standing at the edge of the water and doubtfully eyeing us, or on the bank above staring with a distant gaze at the strange apparition floating down river. After a while the river often descended a gravelly shallow with a rush, and we swiftly floated along past rapidly receding banks of sand or clay. Then, by and by, the river flowed smoothly between green banks under arching trees, and moving thus in state, touched a high hill on the left and passed under a very picturesque, old-fashioned, weather-stained road bridge, perhaps the connecting link of the old Lancaster-Concord turnpike. The river then still softly flowed in beautiful reaches, and after a while at intervals poured darkly with a deep, strong current past great banks of sand, which made a very picturesque feature of the riverscape. They were, for the most part, fringed along the semi-circular top edge with pines, while the sandy façade presented a grotesque spectacle of trees and shrubs engaged in a hopeless struggle to maintain their position in the sliding mass. Plaintively they turned in every direction, while others, settled at the margin of the water, were awaiting with melancholy resignation their hour of doom at the hands of a spring freshet.

After we had journeyed about an hour in all, a shower came up and we made fast to the bank in a leafy cave formed by the drooping branches of a graceful elm, where we were amply protected, while outside the swiftly moving surface of the water boiled with the thickly pattering drops of rain. While waiting for the rain to cease, we had lunch. The clouds finally began to blow over, and we forthwith again got under way, and, ere long, the last rack disappeared and the sunshine, pouring down from a clear sky, filled all the valley with brilliantly luminous light. The river then soon began to wind in a labyrinthian maze over a wide intervale, turning indeed in most capricious fashion hither and thither, as if it had lost its way. The reaches curled round and round, one into another, and at brief intervals we faced every point of the compass. Luckily there was a good current most of the time. After a while, however, the river seemed to be moving in a northerly direction, and we passed through many long, wide reaches, where trees lined the banks almost continuously. Here the Nashua was indeed a lotus-like stream, and, as we pursued our course close to shore under the branches which drooped over the water in a sleepy way, it was easy to fall into a dreamful mood, while the stillness of the scene, the quiet flow of the river, and the gentle rocking of the boat, all contributed to lull one's senses to a dumb feeling of enjoyment. Unless, indeed, I am very much mistaken, some one did fall asleep.

At length the river approached a high hill on the east

and we swung under a bridge of the Worcester and
Nashua Railroad, and put ashore at the east end of the
road bridge, which spans the river at the head of the next
bend below. The dépôt of Still River Village is only
a few steps away. The village however, is half a mile

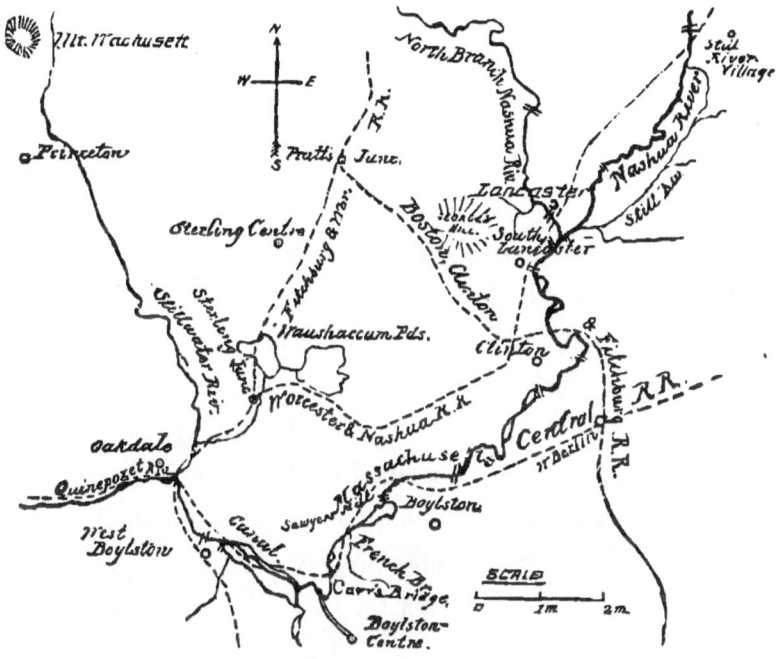

distant on top of the hill, and is reached by a direct, but
pretty steep road. The view along the way, and especially
near and at the summit, however, amply repays the
trouble of ascent. The valley of the Nashua below is
wide and deep, and stretches away a magnificent vista
towards the southwest. Opposite are broad, high hills,

and behind them hilltops roll away until lost in the distance. The Nashua makes a wide semi-circular sweep from West Boylston to Still River Village, which is well indicated by the relative change in position of Wachusett. At West Boylston, Wachusett stands out a sharp cone in the north, while at Still River Village, elongated into slopes of exquisite gracefulness, it bounds the western horizon. The view northward, which terminates with the blue peak of Monadnock, is also very fine.

The few houses of Still River Village are grouped about a triple cross-road on the crown of a hill, where the suns of summer and the winds of winter have the freest access. 'T is a quiet place, as befits its name, which it derives, I suppose, from a sluggish stream that somewhere meanders over the intervale below. As we walked along the deserted roads, not a soul in sight and the only sound the harmonious clang of a blacksmith's hammer on anvil, it seemed indeed as if we had come to a Dreamthorpe in Arcadia. Still River Village, however, boasts a post-office, which we discovered, after a long search, in the wood-shed attached to a private house. The office was equipped with a single row of open boxes affixed to the wall. In one was a paper and in another a letter, which, it is to be hoped, were not soon taken away.

We got under way again about four o'clock, and pulled at a leisurely pace through a succession of lazily winding reaches. We were once startled for a moment by the sound of a stone plumping into the water quite near us. We were only splashed, but nevertheless set up an outcry which speedily brought a farmer through the bushes on the bank with an apology of his complete ignorance of our presence, which was, no doubt, the entire truth. After rowing about an hour in all, we landed at the head of an abrupt bend of the river on the right, and procured some supplies at a farm-house just above.

The river had before been moving generally eastward, but here took a turn in a westerly direction until it laved a hill where the remains of stone abutments were visible on both sides of the river. The reaches were all quite long, and after pulling past the ruins of an old dam we entered one of great length and beauty. The banks on either side were high and lined with trees, and away at the end where the river disappeared in a curve to the right was a great bank of sand and above it an open grove of lofty pines. We landed beneath their shade alongside a fallen tree, and clambering up the sandy slope found the ground above smooth as a house-floor and covered with a matting of pine pins softer to foot-fall than Moquette or Axminster. The water in the long reach through which we had just come, smooth as glass, reflected clouds and sky as in a mirror. Just below, the river descended with a rush by a high clay-bank, while a brook, which goes by the euphonious title of Catacoonamaug, poured with a loud roar over a stony channel along one side of the grove and emptied into the Nashua half-way down the rapid. We pitched the tent in an open space near the edge of the bank, where the canvas gleamed almost sacrilegiously white in the solemn shade of a forest aisle, which ended in darksome recesses; while the sunlight streamed above the tops of the trees and fell like a benediction upon a quaint old farm-house on the ridge of a hill which slopes up with gentle inclination from the opposite bank. The Fitchburg Railroad runs along the hills on the westerly side of the river. We heard from time to time the roar of a train, and occasionally caught sight of a puff of smoke. We could plainly hear the trains slowing to a stop at Shirley Village, about a mile back of us through the woods, and also the strokes of the town clock which rang out the hours in long, musical tones. A path led among the pines to the village, but somehow we did not get there, and Shirley Village remains the Carcassonne of the trip.

We got under way about eight o'clock next morning. We had considerable trouble in getting under a barbed wire stretched across the stream just at the foot of the rapid. The river was quite swift in several places below and at times shallow. We pulled along the east bank to keep out of the sun's rays. While rowing by the mouth of a shallow bayou we discovered a huge snapping turtle in full flight for the river. The oarsman endeavored to stop his progress with an oar, but after turning him over and dancing him on his head several times, the water got riled, and in the confusion he escaped. After rowing about two miles we pulled under a bridge, the road east from which leads to Ayer Junction, and just below shot through a little fall of water amid the ruins of an old dam. The river then flows with an occasional ripple to the bridge of the Fitchburg Railroad, under which it pours in quite a swift rapid. We landed near one end of it on the right and walked to Ayer Junction, which is three fourths of a mile from the river. The convergence of several railroads gives the village an air of considerable importance. What a relief, though, upon returning, to leave the hard bed of the railroad with its confusing series of cross-ties and long lines of glistening rails, and once more embark on the cool river and swing with the flow of a stream gently winding between green banks in a craft responsive to every stroke of the oar! We pulled along one or the other bank in the current, now past a shore lined with bushes and often under overhanging trees. Beyond, on either side, was a pleasing variety of scenery, a wooded hill near or afar off, a grove of pines, or a cultivated field, all quiet and seemingly asleep in the heated noonday air. The river alone gave sign of life, but it too finally made its way lazily amid the tranquil scenes around.

We pulled perhaps an hour, and then landed on the left bank and spread our blankets at the edge of a sunken road at the foot of a steep, thickly wooded hillside. A stream of crystal water sparkled across the road a short distance away, and above was the embankment of a dam and a curious old saw-mill. Below the mill was a small, shallow pond, which was, however, the favored abode of a multitude of frogs, among whom, with the willing aid of a friendly urchin, we made sad havoc in the course of the afternoon, and had an extra *entrée* of rare delicacy, in spite perhaps of mottled associations, for supper.

We got under way again late in the day, and soon pulled under a road bridge, then past the mouth of Squannacook River, and under the bridge of the Peterborough and Shirley Railroad just below, and thence in a succession of long, straight reaches to the Red Bridge at Groton. We landed about a third of a mile below the bridge, and pitched the tent on the high right bank at the edge of a grove of pines. The camp-fire, after dark, lighted up the dense array of trees with startling shadows, and when it was suffered to die away, we were in the midst of a scene desolate in the extreme. Below, the river was still and dark; opposite, flat fields rising in slopes of gentlest inclination, stretched drearily away to a sky-line of black clouds; overhead, a few stars brightly twinkled amid the spray of the motionless black pine boughs, but elsewhere there was no light nor any sound, save the distant croaking of a frog, or, at a rare interval, the dull rumble of a team across the bridge above, and we therefore gladly lost ourselves in slumber.

CHAPTER III.

GROTON. — NASHUA.

WE pulled back to the Red Bridge early on the morrow, and then walked to the village of Groton, which is about a mile from the river. The road leads up a hill, which rises in long and easy slopes, to a road called Farmer's Row, which runs north and south along the edge of a wide plateau. On the wall bordering the Row, a stone has been placed, by Mr. James Lawrence, near his residence, which bears the following inscription: "Near this spot, three children, Sarah, John, and Zacariah Tarbell were captured by the Indians, June 20, 1707. They were taken to Canada, where the sister was placed in a convent. The brothers became chiefs of the Coughnawago tribe, and were among the founders of St. Regis, where they have descendants now living." From Farmer's Row there is a magnificent view, westward, over the valley of the Nashua, which is very wide but quite shallow. The hills fade away in receding masses of green, the outermost circle set with a rim of blue mountains which shoot up here and there into little peaks, in a way unique and extremely picturesque; while Monadnock, in the north, and Wachusett, in the west, dominate still all the landscape. From Farmer's Row, the principal part of the village presents a very fine appearance, on slightly rising ground on a street which runs to the eastward of the Row, and nearly parallel with it. The houses, many of which are almost concealed in the midst of trees, extend in a long, irregular line beneath a heavy bank of dark-green foliage, above which rises, here and there, a church-spire, pointing heavenward.

Proceeding northerly, along the Row, a street leads to the right into the Main Street of the village. Near the junction of the streets is the old burying ground. On the side street, just before going to the Main Street, is the house wherein Margaret Fuller was born and passed her girlhood days. Then proceeding south, one comes to the post-office, and in the same building is the town library. Nearly opposite, is the residence of ex-Governor Boutwell; and in rear thereof, and not far distant, is an eminence called Gibbet Hill, from a tradition that an Indian was executed there. The summit commands a very fine view. Then one comes to the buildings of Lawrence Academy on the left-hand side, while nearly opposite is a row of old houses, one of which, at present occupied by a dealer in old furniture, was built nearly two hundred years ago; and there are several other houses, equally old, in other parts of the town.

On the same street, which is bordered on both sides by beautiful elms of massive growth, is the old tavern, the Central House, which was used as a residence before the

Revolution; and farther down the road is the site of the house, marked by a stone bearing a suitable inscription, wherein William Prescott, the commander of the American forces at the battle of Bunker Hill, was born: and near at hand, is a fine, large, old-fashioned house, which was, at one time, a boarding school, and attended by Margaret Fuller.

Whoever, however, desires to know about Groton should consult the histories of the Hon. Samuel A. Green, ex-mayor of Boston, a native of Groton, who has made a complete collection of the epitaphs in the burying ground, the early town records, and written a History of Groton During the Indian Wars, besides compiling much other miscellaneous information of an interesting character, about the old taverns and stage lines, for instance. There is also a very good history of the town by Caleb Butler.

Groton had very much the same experience as Lancaster in the Indian Wars. The town was settled in 1655, and was in no way molested until an attack, which was made during King Philip's War, March 16, 1676. The inhabitants, however, alarmed by the fate of Lancaster, had retired to the garrison houses, five in number, the sites of which are still known, and were situated, four at least, near the present Main Street. One garrison was taken, but only three persons were lost. Nearly all the buildings of the settlement were destroyed, however, including the meeting-house, the site of which has also been recently indicated by a monument. Soon after the attack, however, the inhabitants abandoned the place, and remained away nearly two years before they ventured to return. They were subject still to alarms from time to time, however, and an occasional assault and depredation, and, during King William's War, an attack was made July 27, 1694, in which twenty or more persons were killed and a dozen or more taken into captivity.

Not far south of the post-office a road leads off from Main Street and, after running westerly over the plateau, terminates on Farmer's Row, just south of the road up from the Red Bridge.

It is supposed that just above the bridge on the west side of the river was the site of an Indian village, as a number of stone implements have been found there near the bank of the stream; and the site of other Indian villages has been indicated in the same way in other places in the town. Dr. Green has quite a large collection of the crude utensils used by the Indians, which have been gathered in various parts of the town, in the rooms of the Massachusetts Historical Society, in Boston.

We returned to the boat about eleven o'clock, and were soon under way. After skirting the high east bank which makes a long curve to where we encamped, we continued on in a good current. By and by the banks were, for the most part, covered with a riotous growth of bushes and above were almost continuously lined with trees, mostly pines. It seemed indeed much of the time as if we were on a river of wildernesses.

We pulled up after a leisurely row of about an hour, perhaps less, under Fitch's Bridge, which was fastened to the banks by two long cables. The road east leads to Groton, which is about two miles distant. The road, however, branches on the way, the southerly road terminating, after a course a little more roundabout than the other, in the village, while the other intersects the Great Road, so called, a road of unusual width, formerly the old stage route, which runs direct from the village to Tileston and Hollingsworth's paper mills, and is there continued over the river on a bridge designated Emery's Bridge on an old map, though I think that now-a-days it is generally spoken of as the Paper Mill Bridge. From this, the third and last bridge in Groton, it is about a mile — a pretty long one, however — by the Great Road to the village.

The road west from Fitch's Bridge likewise branches into two, one of which, well shaded with great maples, runs north parallel with the river, and the other disappears around the spur of a hill and runs, I know not where.

We obtained some supplies at a farm-house, prettily located on the lower road, and had a season of idleness under the maples and on the bridge. After a while we embarked again and pulled through the reaches and then landed on the low, open, left bank, and had lunch under a mammoth oak, which was partly surrounded at a respectful distance by a large family of small trees. The river in front was motionless, as if it too were quietly enjoying a rest. The bank opposite was also low, and beyond were broad and fertile meadows which terminated against pretty, dark-green hills.

When we started on it was about three o'clock. As we rowed along we heard the noise of machinery, which grew louder and louder, and, ere long, we pulled under the Paper Mill Bridge which was being painted a very effective red, and came close to the edge of a dam just below as water was not pouring over. We could not get by on the right, however, as Tileston and Hollingsworth's paper mills covers the bank between the bridge and the east end of the dam, so we pulled to the west shore and landed there on the bulkhead. It would have been easy to make a carry thence along the bank, but, having first unloaded the baggage, we lowered the boat over the dam and moored her at the edge of the flooring below, and in a few minutes the baggage was tossed down, stowed, and we were drifting along in deep water with a rapid current. Before fully getting under way we passed several women in a group on the bank, who looked, in flowing dresses, much like Greek goddesses of Hibernian descent.

Just below where the dam now stands there used to be a shallow place in the river called Stony fordway. Here, on May 8, 1709, John Shattuck, one of the selectmen of the town of Groton, and his son, while crossing the river, were killed by the Indians, and recently a stone has been erected by Messrs. Tileston and Hollingsworth, near the mill, in commemoration of the event.

The last man killed by the Indians in Groton was one John Ames, who was slain on the west side of the river, not far from the bridge, July 9, 1724. The Indian who killed him was, however, slain almost immediately afterward by Ames's son.

On the east side of the Hollis Road, perhaps a mile and a quarter from the village, was the site of a house which has recently been marked by a monument bearing the following inscription: "Here dwelt William and Deliverance Longley, with their eight children. On the twenty-seventh of July, 1694, the Indians killed the father and mother and five of the children and carried into captivity the other three." Of these children, one, Lydia, was sold to the French and placed in a convent, became a Catholic, and died at the age of eighty-four; one perished of hunger and cold soon after his capture; while the other, after remaining with the Indians four years, was ransomed against his will and afterward lived and died in Groton, and his remains now repose in the old burying ground.

The scenery along the river below the paper mills is very fine. We passed two or three rush-lined bays, thick with lily-pads, and a sheltered cove, whose dark expanse was dotted with a countless array of yellow lilies; and now and then a few fragrant white pond-lilies which bloomed, however, at rare intervals along the river border. Here and there along the turfy banks stood a great elm in stately dignity, while on either hand were broad, fertile intervales and hills near or remote. Occasionally we passed a group of lofty trees, and farther down innumerable squads of pines.

After rowing about an hour the river began to grow wider and quite sluggish, and was often bordered with sedges. By and by we came to a small but very graceful islet, covered with trees, at a bend of the stream. On the right is a high, broad hill, bordered at the north by a dense forest of pines, which approaches the river nearly opposite the islet. We then passed through a slight rapid, and thereafter kept along the east shore in a considerable current in the shadow of pines which line the bank almost continuously to Pepperell.

We pulled through the reach, which is quite long and straight, with houses of the village in view at the foot of it, and landed just above the west end of the dam, and then, from the bridge which crosses the river just below, examined the dam to see how we could best get around it. The east bank is high and wellnigh impossible of access. One might indeed get a boat over at the east end of the dam itself if water was not pouring over, as there is a ledge of rocks below there sufficiently high to give footing. It would, however, apparently be an undertaking of doubtful value, as it would have been difficult to navigate the river below when water was pouring over the dam at full head, on account of rocks and shallows. We were, in addition, informed that there is another dam only a short distance farther down. The second dam is quite low, but we concluded upon the whole that it would be better to make a carry to the lower mill, a distance of about quarter of a mile in all; and we therefore had a man take the boat on a wheelbarrow, while we followed with the baggage.

We had not proceeded far, muffled with parcels of various kinds, when a rapid succession of hollow splashings fell upon our ears, and almost ere we realized the nature and occasion of the mishap we found a couple of dozen eggs, which had escaped through the dampened bottom of a paper bag, strewing the hard walk at our feet, and a woman, previously screened from observation behind a pair of blinds, thereupon laughed aloud. The impulse, however, that moved her to merriment was, I assure her, very pardonable, and if the accident pleased

Bridge at Pepperell

the fair — I hope she was fair — *incognita*, I am sure the incident amused us.

We launched the boat in the tail-race in the yard of the mill and were soon speeding in a swift current along the western shore of the river. We soon landed, however, at the covered bridge, a huge, gloomy, cavernous structure.

with very picturesque surroundings, especially about the western mouth.

Here, and on other occasions while in the vicinity, we heard a strange gibberish issuing out of the mouths of boys and young maidens, in which we finally distinguished sounds like hashee and tuthashee, which gave a key to a dialect that, I believe, has some affinity to the Latin tongue. A sentence sounded thus: —

"I wuv-o-nun-dud-e-rug wuv-hash-e-rug-e tut-hash-e-y a-rug-e gug-o-i-nun-gug wuv-i-tut-hash tut-hash-e bub-o-a-tut!"

This language, which, after all, is simply an extension of English, is formed by doubling each consonant and placing the vowel u between the two, except certain consonants whose sound will not permit, as c, which becomes caus to distinguish it from k, and h, which becomes hash, j, jug, r, rug, and w, wuv; while q and x and the vowels remain the same. Pronounced as the youth of Pepperell pronounced it, trippingly on the tongue, with the rapidity of great familiarity, it had a sound as foreign and unintelligible as the speech of Greek or Choctaw. If only the oft-recurring "hash" could be changed into a form a little less flat and discordant, the flow of the utterance would be, from the constant repetition of the most euphonious of vowels, as musical as Tuscan Italian, or the Spanish of Castile.

Pepperell was set off from Groton and given the name

of Pepperell in honor of Sir William Pepperell, who commanded the New England expedition of six thousand men that captured Louisburg and subjected the Isle of Cape Breton to the possession of Great Britain, in 1745. The principal village, which is called Middle Pepperell, is about a mile from the river. The village along the west side of the river by the mills is called Babbatasset, which was the Indian name of the locality. East Village is situated along the Nissitisset, a stream which empties into the Nashua a short distance below the covered bridge, while opposite Babbatasset is the Dépôt Village, as it is called thereabouts, though it appears on maps as East Pepperell.

We encamped about half a mile down river on the left bank under a canopy of pines. We broke camp late in the afternoon of the next day, and drifted quite swiftly along in a strong current, and occasionally were hurried onward by a rapid. The banks were quite high and almost continuously lined with trees. After a while the river grew broader and we passed several quite high sand bluffs. We rowed about an hour altogether, and then landed on the right bank, and at a house above, the first we had seen, made inquiry as to our whereabouts. The woman who gave us directions said she saw our boat coming round the bend above and for a moment thought it was a canoe in which her son was making a voyage home from Canada. He had intended to come down the Passumpsic into the

Connecticut, and paddle down the Connecticut to Miller's River, and up Miller's River as far as possible, which, I should say, could not be very far, — and then, making a carry by the Fitchburg Railroad, launch his canoe in the North Branch of the Nashua, and so reach home, — an interesting journey I hope he successfully accomplished.

Around the next bend below the place where we landed, is a covered bridge, high above the water. The bed of the river underneath is quite thickly strewn with rocks. We had some trouble threading our way among them, but at length came to a shallow channel on the left through which we towed the boat. It would be easy to shoot a little fall the river makes on the right were it not that the water just below dashes with great violence against a rocky ledge. We afterward heard it stated that the Nashua Manufacturing Company intends soon to erect a dam here. There is a small settlement at the east end of the bridge, which is colloquially known as Pumpkin Town. The road west from the bridge leads to Hollis, which is about three miles distant. It is one of the earliest settlements in New Hampshire, and, I am informed, still preserves marks of its antiquity. We pitched the tent on the right bank of the bend next below the falls, as night was falling upon the shadowy landscape.

We were under way again early Monday morning and

rowed along the east bank in a fair current, and for a long time in the shadow of quite an extensive wood. Wild roses and flowers of various hue bloomed at frequent intervals along shore, and the air was full of invigorating freshness. By and by we passed an island of comely proportions, covered with rich undergrowth, and woods, and fields in constant succession. While rowing along we amused ourselves for a time by blowing soap-bubbles. The rainbow-hued globes, instead of bursting when they touched the water, as we supposed they would, glanced lightly along even where it was calm, or gayly bounded from wave to wave, usually a long time before flashing out of sight. Occasionally a bubble mounting in air, moved quickly to the impulse of every variable wind hither and thither until, like its companions on the water, the brilliant iridescence burst into nothingness.

After about an hour's pull we came to Mine Run, the last fall in the river above Nashua. Below the dam at the head of the run was a dry bed of naked jagged rocks which curved downward out of sight between steep banks covered with dreary pines, and all the valley below was a silent sea of green spray. A carry in the rough channel to the head of the river would have been long and difficult, so we rowed over a boom of logs and carried the boat around the gate-house at the right and launched her in the canal below, which, however, at once broadened out into a wide reservoir, bordered with trees except at the end below where it is scarred by a great bank of sand which glistened in the sun. We lingered some time in the open space by the gate-house and in the woods around the head of the reservoir, amid a strange solitude, undisturbed, except by the noise of the water, which struggled out from under the gate, and, at brief intervals, moaned like some monster in distress.

When we embarked and put off into the reservoir we

Main St. Bridge Nashua

were for a while in much doubt which way to proceed. We pulled, however, along the northern shore and at length discovered the head of the canal which was screened from view around a bend, and enjoyed very much our pull through the long, uniform reaches that gently curved one into another between tree-lined banks. The canal is wide and deep, and the water runs along through it in heavy volume with strong current. The canal is dug along the side of a hill and near the end is quite high above the river, which lies in peaceful quiet in the valley below. After a delightful sail of nearly two miles in all, we landed at a carriage-gate on the road which runs along the outer enbankment of the canal, and, carrying the boat across the road, lowered her down the steep bank on the other side, and in a few minutes launched her once more on the Nashua. We pulled up river a short distance and pitched the tent in a piece of woods on the grounds of the Nashua Manufacturing Company, which extend for three miles between the canal and river.

During the night we were awakened by a terrific clap of thunder, which was followed by dazzling flashes of lightning, and a furious thunder storm burst upon us. The wind was so violent that we were for a time apprehensive that it would demolish the tent, which had been less securely fastened than usual, but fortunately the canvas stood up under it, and we escaped a wetting.

We embarked for our final pull Tuesday morning at an early hour. We rowed through quite a long reach past a wooded bank on the right, which, after a while, receded around a deep recess; while opposite were broad fields with hills beyond, and before us was the tall brick chimney of a mill, and here and there amid green slopes the steeple of a church and houses of Nashua. We soon pulled around an abrupt bend, wooded on the left, while opposite, a little farther down the reach below, was the long, high, imposing mill of the Nashua Manufacturing Company, and our way was then in the midst of the city. At the end of the reach, which is lined on the south side with mills and on the north with dwellings, is a long bridge. There is a dam just below Nashua which supplies motive power to the

Junction of Nashua and Merrimac

Jackson Mills, and it is only a short distance below the mill to the Merrimac. We landed at Boynton's boathouse, No. 46 Front Street, whence it is only a few minutes' walk to the dépôt of the Boston and Lowell Railroad, which is near the north end of the bridge.

It is thirty-seven miles by rail from West Boylston to

Nashua, but it is safe to say that the distance by river is at least sixty. The trip occupied a week, but we were actually in the boat rowing only about thirty hours in all. There is indeed an almost constant temptation to linger along the delightful course of the gentle Nashua, and at the end one could not, I think, well help indulging a regret that the voyage had changed from a reality to a dream.

www.ingramcontent.com/pod-product-compliance
Lightning Source LLC
Chambersburg PA
CBHW031451160426
43195CB00010BB/930